al fresco

Inspired Ideas *for* Outdoor Living

JULIE POINTER ADAMS

Artisan | New York

Library of Congress Cataloging-in-Publication Data

Names: Adams, Julie Pointer, author.
Title: Al fresco / Julie Pointer Adams.
Description: New York, NY : Artisan, a division of Workman Publishing Co., Inc. [2022] | Includes index.
Identifiers: LCCN 2021048142 | ISBN 9781648290824 (hardcover)
Subjects: LCSH: Entertaining. | Outdoor living spaces.
Classification: LCC TX731 .A325 2022 | DDC 642/.4—dc23/eng/20211120
LC record available at https://lccn.loc.gov/2021048142

Design by Hallie Brewer

Photographs by Julie Pointer Adams, except on pages 206, 207, 209-11 by Allegra D'Agostini; pages 130–32, 250, 251, 253, 255 by Sophie Davidson; pages 304, 305, 307–9 by Amelia Fullarton; pages 50–51, 53–55 by Olivia Rae James; pages 38, 39, 41–43, 83, 120–23, 170, 177, 212, 214, 232, 234, 235, 237, 238, 241, 256, 291, 298, 300 by Amy Merrick; pages 58, 59, 61 by Camille Moir; and pages 264, 299, 302, 303 by Philip Shelley.

Artisan books are available at special discounts when purchased in bulk for premiums and sales promotions as well as for fund-raising or educational use. Special editions or book excerpts also can be created to specification. For details, contact the Special Sales Director at the address below, or send an e-mail to specialmarkets@workman.com.

For speaking engagements, contact speakersbureau@workman.com.

Published by Artisan
A division of Workman Publishing Co., Inc.
225 Varick Street
New York, NY 10014-4381
artisanbooks.com

Artisan is a registered trademark of Workman Publishing Co., Inc.

Printed in China on responsibly sourced paper
First printing, April 2022

10 9 8 7 6 5 4 3 2 1

For Ryan and Ollie,
my everyday sunshine

MY SON, OLLIE, RUNNING THROUGH THE DUNES AT ONE OF OUR

FAVORITE ESCAPES ALONG THE CENTRAL COAST OF CALIFORNIA

CONTENTS

PREFACE

I have spent most of my life dipping into the cold waters of the Pacific, but the Saint John River running through New Brunswick, Canada, was my first love: Long, clear days basking on its rocky beach or in our green rowboat; gusty afternoon winds whistling through the trees; the sad song of the loon at dusk. Unending days spent outside in every form of far northeastern midsummer weather. Picking wild blueberries, running through the woods, digging for night crawlers so we could fish on drizzly mornings, eating burgers on the deck for dinner. Seeing lightning bugs with the moonrise if we were lucky. These are the memories seared in my mind from returning again and again to the same sacred river retreat that my maternal family has been drawn back to for generations.

Even apart from my semiannual weeks at the river, the natural world has forever been full of bounty for me. When I was growing up, we spent our free time going to nature preserves, bird refuges, lakes, and national parks, or just playing in our backyard, but that world is also where I've always chosen to be alone. As a child, I'd find a sheltering tree or a tucked-away spot in the bushes and retreat on my own. I had fantasies about secret gardens and

other places I could disappear to, away from anyone's watchful eyes. In my independent years, I've more often escaped to open spaces—the ocean, meadows, a sandy riverside—places where I can think, watch, read, listen. Be. Finding deep solace within the natural world, alone, has always given me the ability to be more fully present in moments of togetherness.

On childhood family excursions or those long riverside days, meals were most often an afterthought (at least for me, until perhaps my teenage years), but there were always sandwiches, snacks, picnic baskets, and liters of ginger ale. Being outdoors, with some sort of food, has felt like the most relaxed, restorative way to be together for as long as I can remember. Friends from every facet of my life can all attest that I love a good picnic spread and a long, uninterrupted afternoon outside in which to enjoy it. That's because I believe that whatever way you share that food or drink—at a table, arranged on a blanket, or simply in your lap—it becomes an invitation and a connector, no matter where you are or whom you're with. Food is the magic that greases the rusty wheels of social awkwardness or dullness or shyness. The shared table has been a recurrent theme throughout my adult life; it's where I find, time and time again, that our differences fall away and our commonalities converge. If nature opens us up to ourselves, the food we share opens us up to each other.

What I've also discovered is that my time spent outdoors has produced some of the richest moments in relationships, and the most vivid memories, full of colors, sounds, and smells. There's an intimacy shared in nature that you rarely find elsewhere—I think nature, in her own way, gives us back our truest selves and allows us to share those selves with others. Our most joyous, awe-filled, childlike selves are released in the outdoors, and we remember how to play again. How to enjoy the sun, the water, the air, and, of course, other people, most purely. I love observing grown-ups revel in nature in a way that makes their ages irrelevant: jumping through the waves, lounging in the grass, savoring a meal for hours under the trees. For years I stood by watching my grandfather slice through the afternoon river chop, windsurfing until he was well into his seventies. Now in his nineties, he still swims daily in the river during the summer. And I won't accept any less than this essential vigor and zest for life—this enduring appetite to partake in Earth's best offerings.

Gathering al fresco with friends or family is still, and always will be, my favorite way to spend time together. I've logged countless hours out-of-doors with the people I hold most dear, and every time, I walk away full of something I can't explain. Being outside in the company of loved ones is the freest way to find wellness; to remain grounded, connected, and rooted to what matters. Such moments are the essential stuff of life, and keep us going during the other more routine, less-enthralling aspects of everyday living. Time spent outdoors is never wasted, especially when spent with those we cherish. No matter what your own version of al fresco living and dining looks like, inviting nature into our daily lives feeds and fuels us in deep, abiding ways unparalleled by anything else.

As I write this, my mother is downstairs listening to recordings of that loon of the northeast—the sweet, mournful sound of a lifetime of summers for her as well. To us both, it is the call of longing for the water, for the wild outdoors, for the gathering of family and friends around food, and endless time spent out under the sky. All of us who know this particular place (or any deep-in-your-soul kind of place, for that matter) are forever trying to feel the way we feel when we are at the river no matter where we are—through wisps of light, a scent carried on the air, the sound of the wind in the trees at a certain time of day. This deep desire for connection to the earth and connection to others will never fade, because it's part of our human fabric. We are made to be together, in nature, *of* nature. We are, after all, from dust to dust.

1958 - TAKING OUT
THE ROWBOAT

1960 - GREAT-UNCLE BERNIE,
AUNT SHIRLEY, MOM, GRAMP

1965 - FIRE AND MARSHMALLOWS

1991 - MY FAMILY: KRISTY, DAD, GRAMP,
KATIE, MOM, AND ME

1984 - THE WHOLE RIVER GANG

My Maple Rosemary Popcorn

I've made this popcorn countless times for picnics, parties, book club meetings, warm evenings on the porch, and rainy movie nights at home. It never fails to please. Plus, it's gluten-free and vegan—perfect for any crowd.

MAKES ABOUT 10 CUPS (110 G)

⅓ cup (70 g) popcorn kernels

2 to 3 tablespoons olive oil or other high-heat oil, such as coconut or avocado, if cooking the popcorn on the stovetop

Extra-virgin olive oil for drizzling

Nutritional yeast (aka brewer's yeast) for sprinkling

⅓ cup (25 g) finely chopped rosemary

Salt

Maple syrup for drizzling

Pop your popcorn. I prefer to use an air popper, as it doesn't require any extra oil, but if you don't have one, a covered pot on the stovetop will do.

To cook the popcorn on the stovetop, coat the bottom of a large heavy pot with the olive or other oil, set it over medium-high heat, and drop in 2 to 5 popcorn kernels; cover the pot. Once these kernels pop, add the rest of the popcorn, cover, and cook until all the kernels have popped.

Transfer the popped popcorn to a large bowl, drizzle lightly with extra-virgin olive oil, and toss to coat as evenly as possible. Sprinkle generously with nutritional yeast to taste, again tossing to distribute it evenly. Stir in the rosemary and season with salt to taste, then lightly drizzle with maple syrup, tossing well. The final product will be slightly sticky.

This is best enjoyed immediately.

MY GRAMP DIVING INTO THE RIVER FOR ONE OF HIS DAILY SUMMER SWIMS

INTRODUCTION

This book is an ode to open-air living. It is about spending time together around food and drink under the sun and clouds, amid the trees—nature surrounding you in all her wonder. It invites you to find joyful reverence in the face of natural beauty, but also the lightheartedness that comes from soaking up the outdoors in the company of loved ones.

I offer this compilation of images, interviews, and recipes to anyone looking for a jolt of nature in their life; to anyone who wishes to spend more time outside, feeling carefree and filled with a sense of well-being. I think we all know, deep in our core, that nature is medicine, but too often we get caught up in the humdrum cycles of our lives. We forget, or postpone, or become too busy for our favorite respites in the wild, whether that means a daily walk to the park, a moment of quiet in the sun, or a laid-back dinner in the backyard. I too am guilty of the excuse of busyness (ironically, never more so than while creating this book), but I always regret that as soon as I return to the freedom of the outdoors.

While you'll find candidly captured examples of, and inspiration for, simple gatherings of all sizes, the aim is not to inspire you toward more styled occasions or fancy tablescapes, intended to be broadcast across social media. In fact, I'd like to propose just the opposite. Do more things in nature and partake in more shared experiences with friends just for yourself and for those with whom you may be enjoying the moment. The goal is to fill yourselves up with all that the outdoors and a rich sense of community can offer you—that's it. Make more meals, pack more picnics, and get outside. It doesn't matter how your spread looks; the point is to just *do it*, whether it's with a can of Pringles or a smorgasbord of specialties. The words, photos, prompts, and more are here to nudge you toward ideas that you can try for yourself, in your own unique way, with your own unique people.

The interviews and ideas shared here are from friends from many different places and walks of life, with varying relationships to the outdoors. The binding element is that all of them have found nature, and spending time in it with others, to be a source of rich and abiding *life*. The kind of life and well-being and contentment we all crave but are not always sure how to find. Nature heals in ways we can only begin to articulate, and much of

the time, that healing is difficult to measure; the ways that trees, plants, wildlife, weather—and so much more—sing to our souls are more often the kinds of expressions reserved for poets. What I find lovely and compelling about everyone here is that the outdoors has markedly changed their tune in life—and they are happy to share their experiences with others in an easy, down-to-earth way.

Each of these friends has provided a recipe they consider a go-to for casual outdoor gatherings. Whether you find the recipes simple or a bit challenging, consider them further ideas for getting you outdoors, with food for sharing. While recipes can be sources of inspiration, though, there's never a need to go all out in order to enjoy a get-together with friends or family. Sometimes the best way is the most fuss-free way—suggest a potluck, order a pizza, or pick up sandwiches en route.

My hope is that these pages push you toward the open air, however that may look for you. The goal is never perfection (who's the judge of that, anyhow?), but simply to get outside and just let your spirit get refreshed. Bringing friends along helps, and food always makes everything better.

WAYS TO GATHER

Here are some no-fuss ways to get together any day of the week. Spontaneous or planned, all of these occasions are instant mood-lifters.

~ Take a hike or a bike ride and bring along a loaf of bread, some cheese, nuts, water, and chocolate to snack on along the way.

~ Meet at the beach, a park, or a river, and pack a mini camp stove and some sausages to cook up for everyone. Pack mustard, and if you can find salty pretzel buns, they are chef's kiss.

~ Invite folks over for a chili taste-off. Cornbread is a must.

~ A potluck is always a winner, no matter where you host or meet up. Sunset picnics with a view are my personal favorite.

~ Eating popsicles on the porch is a fun idea for any warm day. The food never needs to be fancy to guarantee a good time.

~ Backyard happy hour with no cooking required is hard to beat. Cheese, crackers, a bit of salami, olives, grapes, and something special to drink— you've got yourself a party.

~ Meet up at the farmers' market and task everyone with buying something to share. Enjoy a picnic feast together from your bounty.

~ Keep a standing Friday-night date with another couple, your book club group, or your best pals. Switch up where you meet and who's responsible for food so no one gets hangout burnout.

~ Squeeze in an early-morning breakfast and coffee as the sun is rising.

The rhythm of the waves and the vastness
of the sea never get old for me.

—Gina Stovall

GATHERING
BY THE WATER

Being close to water, where water—whether ocean, river, lake, pond, swimming hole, or trickling stream in the woods—meets land and sky always has a calming, grounding effect. Returning to our own special watering hole always feels like a homecoming, however long we've been away. Being around water gives us room to breathe, and to take in our surroundings.

Perhaps that's why gathering near the water for a meal, no matter the size of the group, feels momentous every time. Whether it's sandwiches; a cooler's worth of snacks, like chips and dip; a bowl of cut-up watermelon; or a full-on cookout, this is the kind of everyday celebration we can all use more of. Seeing others enjoy themselves by or in the water, we can't help but want to be there with them. So grab your most versatile blanket, your easiest meal (takeout will do just fine), and whoever's available. The water is waiting.

The different sounds water can make are all deeply grounding and calming to me.

Nicole Wilson

Leo Basica and Taiana Giefer

Fierce lovers of land and sea, Leo and Taiana are slowly building their dream home perched atop the foothills of Montecito, California. Leo does graphic design, and Taiana is a felt artist, model, and community organizer—strategically living and working where they're never more than ten minutes away from catching the next good wave. Leo gives us the lowdown on their daily life together, with Taiana providing the beautiful breakfast surfboard spread shown on the opposite page.

—

Where does your love of the outdoors come from?
We are both lucky to have had parents who loved being outside and appreciated open spaces. When I was growing up, my father was the head of a travel agency in Croatia, and he was always exploring new places around the world. I wanted to follow along. My mother had a passion for fishing and would spend hours sitting on the cobblestone beaches of Croatia looking for shells. As for Taiana, both her parents were and still are nomads, saying yes to any new adventure that comes their way—they are among those people who are truly young at heart and have that sparkle in their eye.

How do you define well-being? What tangible daily acts do you practice to claim it for yourself?
What well-being is to us is always changing. Sometimes just pushing yourself to jump into cold water, enjoying some simple toasted sourdough with butter with no distractions, or having a quiet moment alone walking around the property is enough to feel grounded. A whole body stretch—a head to toe wiggle—here and there does wonders as well.

How has your relationship with the outdoors affected and informed the way you live in your home?
We're currently building our own home, and as we imagine where this window will be and where that shelf should go, we're constantly keeping the outdoors in mind, whether it's the view or streaks of light, or a pine tree or island peek that we want to intentionally frame.

What in nature brings you joy?

The greatest gift of nature for us is the silence. And then a hawk shriek. Silence. And then a wave lapping the shore. It's always changing and endlessly immersive.

What are your favorite rituals around food and eating with others?

We have some friends who religiously lick their plates clean after every meal. Others who always have a cocktail before dinner. For us, it's making sure everyone has plenty of food on their plate and a full glass.

What kind of food or meal do you most enjoy sitting down to?

First thing that came to mind is a loaded farmer's salad with spiced fried chickpeas, lots of green goddess-y dressing, and a sausage, or two. Perfect dinner.

Some beautiful pieces of bread and canned sardines, a sliced Cherokee tomato with some sea salt. Perfect lunch.

Fried egg, avocado, and a little dried salami. Or a bowl of thick yogurt, with some berries and granola. Perfect breakfast.

Dried Kalamata olives (with the pits still in them, of course). Some cheese. Perfect snack.

What's one significant memory or feeling from your childhood connected to eating with others?

The most vivid memories for both of us are a packed house of laughing people, some dancing, some lounging, and the sound of loud music and utensils clinking against plates.

You're both surfers and spend a lot of time in the ocean—what's something that surfing has taught you about the power of nature that you might not have learned otherwise?

A decade ago, we never thought surfing would take us to different parts of the world. Now it's hard to think of traveling without fitting a surf in somewhere along the way.

Both of you came to live in Santa Barbara when you were teens. How has your relationship to the outdoors changed since you began living here?

I came to Santa Barbara to play tennis for UCSB because of how great the weather is year-round, and I ended up staying because the city reminds me so much of my hometown of Makarska—it has the same geography and orientation with the islands and mountain range. Taiana became truly connected to the ocean and surfing after moving here from Los Angeles in middle school. Living up in the hills, being able to walk out of the house and be on a trail right away is truly special.

What gets you most excited in nature?

For me, glassy offshore conditions. For Taiana, taking endless creek dips.

What makes for a really good get-together?

Dinner with just one other couple on a warm night. Veggies and good meat from farmer friends, with a couple of bottles of wine. There's really nothing better. Both of us gravitate to the edges of parties and lean toward having intimate groups over so we can have deep conversations and really catch up with other people. What makes it a great get-together, though, is when the dishes are done before we go to sleep. Waking up not having to clean up is oh-so-nice.

—

Bircher Muesli

This is a classic "everything but the kitchen sink" family recipe. Throw in whatever you've got in the pantry or fridge.

SERVES 6 TO 8

2 apples

1 cup (240 ml) yogurt or kefir

1 cup (240 ml) citrus juice
(use any citrus fruit you have)

½ cup (45 g) quick-cooking oats

TOPPINGS (at least one, or a combination of several)

Fresh fruit—any kind

Dried fruit (we love goji berries)

Nuts and/or seeds

Honey

Bee pollen

Granola

Grate the apples into a bowl. Mix in the yogurt, citrus juice, and oats. Let the mixture sit for about 10 minutes to soften the oats. The timing is loose, as it really depends on how thick or creamy you like your muesli.

Serve with your choice of toppings.

Collections *from the* Outdoors

One sure way to slow down in nature is to notice what's around you, and collect what catches your eye. Here are some things that caught mine.

TINY ROCKS OF SIMILAR SIZE & COLOR

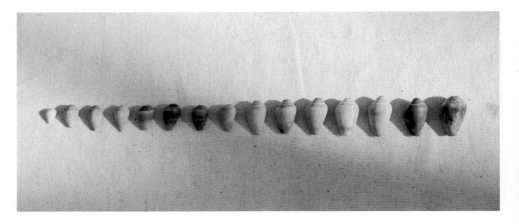

A VERY GRATIFYING GRADATION

UNUSUAL BEAUTIES

ONE PERFECT SHELL & TWO ODDITIES

PERFECT SKIPPING ROCKS OR PAPER WEIGHTS

TOMATILLOS & FAVA BEANS —
NOT MADE TO LAST BUT
DELIGHTFUL WHILE THEY DO

Sharon and Paul Mrozinski

Sharon and Paul split their time between the coastal isle of Vinalhaven, Maine, and the Luberon region of France, finding antique treasures near and far to sell in their Vinalhaven shop, Marston House. Here, Sharon gives us a window onto life at the waterside.

—

Where does your love of the outdoors come from?
My upbringing in Arizona in the desert—as a child, I was free as a bird to wander. Nature has been my lifelong caretaker, best friend, confidant, and guide.

What in nature brings you joy?
The sounds of the water, the wind, and the birds, and the smells of the earth. For us, our walks and the tides running past our island home provide us with all the meditation we need.

How do you define well-being? What tangible daily acts do you practice to claim it for yourself?
Well-being is a lifelong commitment. I was born a mover, and I have always been physically active: swimming, running, walking, and biking are all part of my life. I've added yoga to the mix over the past twenty years, and I cannot live without it. I enjoy ice cream every day—everyone needs a guilty pleasure—but mostly we eat spicy green veggies. Our forty years of love has a lot to do with our well-being too.

How has your relationship with the outdoors affected and informed the way you live in your home?
On our morning walks, we forage for greens and flowers for our big daily salad. I never come home with empty pockets. My "collections" are found and gathered in nature. I pick up stones and dead birch or sumac branches to use as sculptures, and I've covered our walkways with shells of all kinds.

We are working on our teeny-tiny bit of land between us and the rock wall at the water's edge. Paul forages for beach roses, wild peas, and ferns.

What do you find to be the true value of gathering around food with friends?

Communing with friends and family is the most delicious part of a meal for me. We've always enjoyed making meals as a family. All four of our kids are great cooks as a result. When we moved to our 1780s sea captain's home in Maine, we had no stove or oven until early winter. Paul became a grill master, and I became a one-pot-meal expert, with the pot hanging over the fire in the fireplace. With almost no heat on the second and third floors, the fireplace became our gathering spot for everything.

What are your favorite rituals around food and eating with others?

My best memories around meals as a kid were picnics. I still love them best, probably because they are outdoors. Paul did not do picnics growing up, and I work hard to persuade him to enjoy them.

Now we have the opportunity to eat outdoors on our deck over the water on Vinalhaven, and in Bonnieux, with our dining room windows open wide, it's almost as though we are outside. We overlook the water in Maine, and in France we overlook the Luberon hills, so it is close to being on a picnic.

What kind of food or meal do you most enjoy sitting down to?

We fix fresh veggie soup for a late breakfast and a big spicy green salad for a late lunch. We get excited to make them together and share them with each other.

During our busy summer season, Paul prepares the salads for us, and we often eat them sitting out in front of our shop rather than closing for lunch. That has actually become a ritual since moving to Vinalhaven; the locals love seeing us enjoy our lunch on Main Street. When family and friends are dining with us, Paul grills fish, lobster, oysters, chicken, or lamb. I usually slice potatoes, shallots, and heads of garlic, toss them with a little sea salt and olive oil, and throw them into the oven.

You both originally came from drastically different landscapes than that of coastal Maine (Chicago for Paul, the Arizona desert for Sharon)—what drew you to the rugged beauty of this particular island?

I loved growing up in the desert but longed to live in Maine. I was always looking at picture postcards of Maine, with its water, its seasons, and its mountains.

I first visited Maine in 1974, and I had to return. I brought Paul to Maine in 1984, both of us divorced and with two kids each. He loved the early architecture and the classic simple Capes, with wooden clapboards and cedar shingles.

I refer to days that are totally free of obligations and expectations as "free-range" days. How do you two like to spend your free-range days together?

We walk in nature or sit at water's edge reading to each other, feet dangling in that cold salty tidal water, on Vinalhaven. Or we nap on the hills, surrounded by the orchards or the vineyards of the Luberon. I always bring a good old piece of homespun we can lie down on, just in case.

—

Big Lunch Salad

This salad is good at any time. Switch up any of the ingredients depending on what you can find and what local farmers are growing, using whatever is fresh and seasonal and never the same. Preserved lemons can also be used to garnish soups or grilled fish, either chopped or topped as thin, long strips.

Start with the juice of a half lemon in your favorite salad bowl. Add enough good olive oil (nonfiltered if possible) to make a dressing, stirring constantly with a wooden spoon, until emulsified (I count to 12 as I pour the olive oil). Add 4 garlic cloves, minced, or less if garlic frightens you.

Add the following roots and stems to the bowl, stirring briskly to coat.

~ A red beet, or any color beet of your choosing, thinly sliced

~ A radish-sized white turnip, thinly sliced

~ A radish or two (we prefer watermelon radishes, but your choice), thinly sliced

~ A head of broccoli, cut into bite-sized pieces, including thick-sliced stems (our favorite part)

~ A thinnish crosswise slice from a head of red cabbage

Add a few handfuls of the spiciest greens and sprouts you can find and toss well with your wooden salad servers.

Top off your salad with strips of rind from Preserved Lemons (recipe follows), blueberries, and raspberries, or any fruit in season, such as strawberries and sliced or chopped cantaloupe and kiwis. Don't throw away any leftovers—eat them later or the next morning while you're fixing breakfast.

Preserved Lemons

Cut 5 to 7 lemons in half and squeeze out as much juice as possible. Save the juice for another use. Cut the bottoms off the lemon halves, completely removing the pithy parts; you want to use only the cleaned rinds.

With kitchen shears or sharp scissors, cut the lemon halves into ¼-inch-wide (6 mm) pieces, going diagonally across the rind. Transfer to a glass jar with glass lid and rubber seal.

Add 1½ teaspoons kosher salt to the lemons and enough boiling water to cover. Let cool.

Seal the jar and let the lemons stand in a cupboard or other cool, dark place for 4 days or so, then transfer to your fridge and enjoy on most everything.

Gina Stovall

Gina, a former geologist, is the designer of Two Days Off, a carbon-neutral lifestyle brand she developed while still working as a scientist by day. She and her architect partner, Adham, live close to the beach in Los Angeles. Gina shares how she stays grounded amid the busyness of owning and running her own company.
—

Where does your love of the outdoors come from?
When I was a child, my favorite place was Central Park's Conservatory Garden. My parents or grandmother would take me to play at its Burnett Fountain nearly every day after school. I called it my secret garden; I am not sure if I knew at the time that the fountain was named for Frances Hodgson Burnett, author of *The Secret Garden*. After our family moved from New York City to the South, I spent my days playing in the woods, collecting caterpillars, and reading on grassy patches in the sun.

What's your relationship with the sun?
Reverent. Being in the sun is how I recharge and ground myself when life feels hectic. When I was living in New York City in my early twenties, I came to realize that I suffered from seasonal depression, triggered by a lack of sunshine and vitamin D. That was in part why I moved to Southern California, and to this day, I thoroughly take advantage of basking in the sun outside all year round.

What part of, or activity in, the natural world do you find most healing or grounding?
Being on the beach. The rhythm of the waves and the vastness of the sea never get old for me. The beach is the only place where my mind can slow down and I can be present without any effort.

How do you define well-being? What tangible daily acts do you practice to claim it for yourself?
Well-being, to me, is being nourished physically, mentally, and spiritually. I've found that I tend to sacrifice my well-being for the sake of being productive, so I have developed daily practices that force me to check in with

myself each morning. I start my days slowly and never schedule anything before ten o'clock. That way, I have the time to meditate, journal, take a long walk, or just sleep in a bit—whatever my body tells me I need for that day.

How has your relationship with the outdoors affected and informed the way you live in your home?

My concern for the planet, specifically about climate change, heavily influences my lifestyle. I try to buy less and surround myself with only beautifully crafted objects that inspire me whenever I look at them. As I have begun to think holistically about the things I acquire and use daily, I've naturally gravitated toward things with stories and purpose, often made from materials found in nature.

What in nature brings you joy?

The quiet busyness of it all. What goes unseen day-to-day are the processes of plants growing, insects going about their daily routines, winds moving through the landscape. These little miracles bring me so much joy.

What kind of food or meal do you most enjoy sitting down to?

Breakfast on the weekend—slow, and often indulgent.

What's one significant memory or feeling from your childhood connected to eating with others?

I have such visceral memories of my late grandmother serving us fried rice after school. She'd make a huge wok of food and serve it on enormous plates. I always imagined she bought her plates from a special store because they were almost the size of serving platters, and yet only just large enough to accommodate her oversized portions!

How has your background as an earth scientist shifted the way you think about and interact with nature on a daily basis?

I have great respect for nature and natural systems from studying them in so much depth over the years. Humankind works very hard to conquer nature in one way or another, forgetting the fact that we are part of natural systems, not outside of them. I think acknowledging this reality allows me to appreciate my environment more each day.

How did you find your way to being a clothing designer and entrepreneur, running your own company? Was this something you ever imagined doing as a child?

I never envisioned myself as an entrepreneur when I was young. I always figured I'd be a scientist, conducting interesting experiments and doing essential research. As my career progressed, though, I needed to express myself creatively. Eventually what was just a hobby, making my own clothing, became a thought experiment for me. I wondered if there was a way to create sustainable, climate-positive clothing and still make a profit. That experiment became Two Days Off, and I found myself a business owner. Some days I still wonder how I got here, but as I think back, it is no surprise to realize that my curiosity was the catalyst for it all.

How has your own family experience growing up shaped the way you gather with others and what you choose to do outside with friends?

I have a huge family and grew up with lots of siblings and cousins around. So many of my childhood memories are centered on family barbecues, fish fries, and birthdays, almost all taking place outdoors to accommodate all that energy!

—

Rosemary, Mushroom, and Potato Frittata

A frittata is one of my go-to dishes for gatherings or a quick meal. It is easy to make and can be eaten at any time of day, and you can fill it with anything you wish! This one has been a favorite for years because of its heartiness and the mix of sweet and savory flavors. I make a simple green salad to serve with it when I'm feeling fancy.

SERVES 4

½ Vidalia or other sweet onion

8 ounces (225 g) baby bella mushrooms

4 small Yukon Gold potatoes

4 large (200 g) eggs
(5 or 6 if they are smaller)

Salt and pepper

¼ cup (60 ml) milk (optional)

Extra-virgin olive oil

Leaves from a couple rosemary sprigs

To prep your ingredients, thinly slice the onion and slice the mushrooms. Dice the potatoes into ¼- to ½-inch (6 to 13 mm) cubes.

Whisk the eggs in a medium bowl and season with salt and pepper. For a fluffier frittata, add the milk (I often skip it).

Heat a 9-inch (23 cm) cast-iron or other ovenproof skillet over medium heat. Add a tablespoon or so of olive oil, then add the onions and slowly caramelize them.

Once the onions are caramelized, add the mushrooms and sauté until tender. Season lightly with salt. Transfer the onion and mushroom mixture to a plate and set aside.

Add a bit more olive oil to the pan, and once it is hot, add the potatoes. From here, you can add up to half a cup (120 ml) of water, a little at a time, and keep the pan covered until the potatoes are tender throughout. Uncover, then add the rosemary and salt to taste and allow the potatoes to brown on at least one side.

Preheat the broiler. Add the onion and mushroom mixture to the pan and stir to distribute everything evenly. Add your whisked eggs to the pan; do not stir. Cook, still over medium heat, for 5 minutes, or until the frittata is almost set. Finish your frittata under the broiler for a few minutes, until the top begins to lightly brown.

Voilà! It's done. Let cool a bit and cut into wedges to serve.

Olivia Rae James
Suárez and
Blake Suárez

Olivia, Blake, and their young daughter, Agnes, fully enjoy the essence of a close-to-nature life in Charleston, South Carolina, where Olivia is a lifestyle and wedding photographer and Blake is a graphic designer.

—

Where does your love of the outdoors come from?
Blake: My parents did a wonderful job introducing my sister and me to the outdoors at a very young age, whether it was through books or actual experiences. They are very much "leave it better than you found it" folks, so any time spent outside was also a quick lesson in caring for Mama Earth. We grew up in southwestern Miami, close to the Everglades, so our time was filled with exploring wetlands and mangroves, climbing trees and catching tadpoles, surrounded by alligators and herons of every size and color. Such guidance and exploration were key to setting a strong foundation for the kind of parent I want to be.

What kind of environment or landscape gives you the most joy in life?
Olivia: I feel most at home near the water. My grandpa built our little beach cottage in Nags Head in 1985 and chose our spot on the sound specifically because it has a perfect view of both the sunrises and the sunsets.

B: I'm a sucker for a walk in the salt marsh with a thermos of coffee, especially near the end of Folly Beach in South Carolina. You can tuck in to the grasses and spot the meandering little drain that spits out into three main creeks. There is some fantastic birding there, and you can always catch sight of a dolphin. It's the perfect environment to reflect on both the present and what's to come, because it's a long walk out and back.

What in nature brings you joy?
O: Flowers, fresh air, sunshine, birds, morning light, evening light—and moments of stillness in which to notice it all. Being present with Agnes and seeing the natural world through her eyes brings so much magic to our lives.

What are your favorite rituals around food and eating with others?

O: I love creating a nice ambience for meals—sometimes that means a tablecloth, place settings, and flowers, and sometimes it just means lighting a candle on our kitchen island where we eat on barstools. If we make a point to treat mealtime like an occasion, it becomes one!

What kind of food or meal do you most enjoy sitting down to?

O: We eat super-simple meals based on whatever fresh produce we have from our farm box that week—lots of salads, roasted veggies, pastas. We have a weekly pizza night with Blake's sourdough crust. We top it with just tomatoes, a *ton* of garlic, fresh oregano from our yard, and nutritional yeast—it's our favorite!

What's one significant memory or feeling from your childhood connected to eating with others?

O: When I was growing up, my parents were constantly entertaining and hosting beautiful dinner parties. There was always so much laughter at those dinners, and they sometimes turned into dance parties, with my dad at the piano and all their friends dancing in our foyer.

B: I will never forget how close to one another we always felt at our dinner table. Without fail, we sat down for dinner together, and there were few distractions. I remember that when other relatives visited, we would laugh until our stomachs hurt.

Your family seems to make the most of days spent outside—what kind of rhythms and routines are you enjoying lately as a family of three?

O: During our summers, which we spend in Nags Head, the line between inside and outside is blurred and it feels like we *live* outside. We watch every sunrise and sunset from the dock, go to the beach daily even if it's just for a quick dip in the ocean, and spend countless hours on our dock chatting, eating, and taking in the view.

In Charleston, we start every day with a walk to our neighborhood community gardens and playground. There are so many sweet moments along the way for us—Agnes picks flowers from our front yard to carry with her, waves and "woofs" at every dog we pass, sniffs the blooming jasmine with endless enthusiasm, and leads us in the direction of her favorite mulberry tree. She also loves to point out the different birds we see, and Blake loves teaching her their names.

How has your relationship with the outdoors affected and informed the way you live in your home?

O: Our kitchen opens up to our back porch, which is where we spend most of our time (every season but summer). Early-morning coffee in our lounge chairs, meals with friends around the outdoor table—the porch is definitely the heart of our home.

B: When we first moved into our house, a friend of ours, a horticulturist and planting expert extraordinaire, gave me the idea of scrapping half of our lawn to plant native perennials. This project has been a recurring gift, because we get to experience blooms throughout the year and see spent flowers reseed other parts of the yard. Since then, we've been slowly turning over every patch of grass so we have flowers that fill our views from every window of the house. This transformation has also welcomed a wide chorus of songbirds to our yard, which we enjoy whenever we step outside.

What's your favorite way to gather with friends around food?

O: When I was younger and had no shortage of free time, I used to throw elaborate dinner parties, spending a full day or two cooking and baking, setting the table, et cetera, but these days, I love spontaneous, intimate dinners with just a few friends—long, candlelit evenings when the wine is flowing and we end up talking and laughing late into the night.

B: Nothing beats sharing a couple of beers on the porch, catching up on things that matter—or don't matter—and laughing at nonsense.

—

Roasted Tomato and Garlic Pasta

An infinitely adaptable tomato/garlic/basil pasta dish.

SERVES 2 OR 3

2 heads garlic

Olive oil

4 pints (1 L) cherry tomatoes

Salt

A box of your favorite pasta (we use Banza chickpea pasta)

As much basil as you like, leaves removed from stems

Parmesan cheese or nutritional yeast for serving

Preheat the oven to 400°F (200°C). Remove most of the outer layers of the papery skin from the heads of garlic and slice off the tops so all the cloves are visible. Put the garlic in a small baking dish, drizzle with olive oil, and wrap in aluminum foil. Roast for 45 minutes to 1 hour, until the cloves are very soft. Remove the garlic from the oven and let cool completely in the baking dish. Turn the oven down to 325°F (165°C).

Slice the cherry tomatoes in half. Put them on a rimmed baking sheet lined with parchment paper, lightly drizzle with olive oil, and arrange them cut side down on the pan. Roast for 30 to 45 minutes, until they look slightly wrinkly and deflated. Remove from the oven and let cool completely on the baking sheet.

Now cook the pasta! Bring a large pot of salted water to a boil, add the pasta, and cook until al dente; drain in a colander. If you're using an "alternative" pasta (like chickpea or lentil), be sure to rinse it thoroughly under cold water, or it will get mushy and stick together.

Transfer the pasta to a serving bowl, add a healthy pour of olive oil, and squeeze the softened garlic cloves from their skins. Toss well to combine. Then add the basil (I like to roll the leaves up in a bundle or two and cut them using kitchen scissors). Add the roasted tomatoes and another glug of olive oil if needed. Finish with salt if necessary and Parmesan or nutritional yeast, and serve.

How to Heal in the Sun, Together or Alone

The sun does wonders for our bodies—mentally, spiritually, physically. These are some of my favorite ways to drink in the sun, no matter the season.

~ Sit outdoors in a chair, doing nothing, for long enough to really feel the sun on your skin, and on your eyelids, and warming your core.

~ Stretch every part of your body, from your jaw down to each one of your toes.

~ Drink three glasses of water while standing outside in your bare feet.

~ Let yourself become deeply relaxed, until your body starts to enter a dream state. Coming to consciousness again feels like heaven.

~ Spend ten minutes weeding, getting your fingers into the dirt (or at least onto some plant matter). If you don't have your own yard, volunteer to do a few minutes of weeding or pruning each day for a neighbor who can't get out much.

~ Find a day to dedicate yourself to spending the better part of it outside. It's a total refresh for your whole being.

~ Read in the sun for thirty minutes, no distractions. (If you're anything like me, your child will be nearby; do the best you can.)

~ Drink a cup of tea in the morning sun. Break bread with a loved one.

~ Go somewhere you can really feel the wind. Listen to it and let it flow through you.

~ If you can't be outside, tap into your best cat-like instincts and find the sunniest patch in the house. Fully embrace it and take a nap.

Camille Moir

Camille is a beading artist who is innately conscious of the natural environment, even while living in the inner city of Naarm/Melbourne, in Wurundjeri Country, with her partner, Roslyn, and dog companion, Ru.
—

Where does your love of the outdoors come from?
From my parents. In her twenties, my mum lived in Wytaliba, New South Wales, which is in the bush. She built her own mud-brick house with materials from the land, and planted an orchard of three hundred fruit trees. She is a gardener and a scientific and natural-history artist. She has instilled in me a deep appreciation for and knowledge of native and introduced flora and fauna. My dad is a surfer, maritime worker, and furniture maker. He taught me how to read the waves and weather systems and gave me an appreciation for natural materials—their properties and histories.

How has your relationship with the outdoors affected and informed the way you live in your home?

I have grown to understand that the ways we inhabit our homes connect inherently to the complex environmental systems around us, and that this can be reflected in our use and appreciation of natural materials. I come from a family of woodworkers, so my home is filled with timber and natural furnishings. All our heating is hydronic, and we use rainwater for our garden. We recycle, minimize waste as much as possible, and grow our own fruits and vegetables. Our housemate and longtime friend is a sculptor and jeweler, and he has taught me about metals and stones as well. It's lovely being able to identify the origins of what is around you every day.

What environment or place in your childhood or adolescence shaped you most significantly?
It's hard to pick one environment, as the three most significant adults in my life loved three very different ecosystems—dry bush (the outback), the beach, and wetlands. My mother used to do lots of bush walks, collecting specimens to draw or paint (an eel lived in our bath for a few days once so she could paint it), and

my dad would spend a lot of time surfing and fishing. I used to swim in the ocean on freezing-cold days and fish off the pier down on the Mornington Peninsula or from our tinny (a small tin boat), which was eventually stolen from the shore. My grandma Elaine was a pioneer for saving wetlands, especially Kooyongkoot Creek (also known as Gardiners Creek); *kooyongkoot* translates to "haunt of the waterfowl." As a family, and sometimes alongside botanists and horticulturalists, we would monitor, maintain, and improve the water quality, sowing appropriate plants to enrich the natural filtering systems and animals. My grandma always used to grab on to my hood so I wouldn't fall in as I peered into the creek while we tried to spot the resident water rat. So, maybe I'll conclude that I was very much shaped by being outside!

What are your favorite rituals around food and eating with others?

Each morning, my partner, Roslyn, or I will make coffee to have in bed together before the day begins. I love opening the shutters and seeing what kind of sky the day has brought. We use our favorite coffee mugs (made by our friend, ceramicist Amy Leeworthy) and read the news together or do the weekend quiz, with Ru the dog at our feet.

What do you find to be the true value of gathering around food with friends?

The laughter and the debates. It brings me joy when friends drop by spontaneously and the occasion becomes a full-blown dinner party. We have had a lot of gatherings in our home over many years; it's this type of coming together with friends that builds deep connections that last a lifetime.

Is there a tree, plant, or even general landscape that you feel especially connected to?

Eucalyptus caesia (the Silver Princess eucalyptus), which is an Australian gum tree. Its powdery blue-green leaves are sickle-shaped—designed to catch the wind. Arching branches create scanty dappled patches of light. If you rub or crush the leaves in your hand, the oils produce the characteristic eucalyptus smell of camphor, menthol, sap, and lemon. I just planted a eucalyptus tree in the backyard, and it's sprung up rather swiftly.

What activity, habit, or ritual practiced outdoors makes you feel most fully alive and fully yourself?

Looking up at the night sky in the desert is a way to feel at once close to yourself and connected to what's beyond. It's almost as if you can hear both your body and the surroundings at an equal volume. Dancing is also on par with this. Maybe feeling fully alive is dancing in the desert in the dark?

—

MAYBE FEELING FULLY ALIVE IS
DANCING IN THE DESERT IN THE DARK?

Makrut Steamed Fish with Lime Rice and Papaya Salad

This recipe is my favorite to cook, and you can take it outdoors wrapped in its banana leaf for lunch. If you are in a rush, you can replace the makrut lime rice with plain jasmine rice. You could also use some fish sauce for seasoning instead of salt. Dress it all with lots of fresh coriander!

SERVES 4

MAKRUT LIME RICE

2 cups (380 g) jasmine rice

1½ cups (355 ml) coconut water

1½ cups (355 ml) water

Pinch of salt

1 teaspoon palm sugar

7 makrut lime leaves, 4 left whole, 3 finely chopped

2 pandanus leaves, tied in knots (these can be found in Asian grocers, but the dish can be made without them if need be)

A 2-inch (5 cm) piece galangal, bruised or scored with a knife and cut into eight ¼-inch (6 mm) slices (reserve 4 slices for the fish on the opposite page)

1 stalk lemongrass, bruised

3 roots from cilantro sprigs

To prepare the rice, rinse it in a sieve and soak in water to cover for an hour or two.

Drain the rice and put it in a heavy-bottomed pot. Stir in the coconut water and water, then add the salt, sugar, all of the makrut lime leaves, the pandanus leaves, 4 slices of the galangal, the lemongrass, and the cilantro and stir again. Bring to a boil over medium-high heat, then cover, reduce the heat to low, and cook for 15 minutes, or until the rice is tender. Turn off the heat and let rest for 5 minutes. Remove the galangal.

Meanwhile, prepare the fish: Wave the banana leaves over an open gas flame until they develop a waxy, shiny finish. Lay one banana leaf in a steamer basket, then lay 2 fish fillets on it and garnish them with 2 makrut lime leaves, 2 half lemongrass stalks, 2 pieces of galangal, and 2 cilantro roots. Fold the edges of the leaf over to enclose the fish; this doesn't need to be a supertight wrap, just enough so the flavors won't escape as the fish steams. Repeat with another banana leaf, if using, the other 2 fillets, and the remaining garnishes. Steam for 3 minutes, or until the fish is just cooked through. Remove the galangal.

To make the salad, combine the garlic, salt, and chilies in a big mortar and pound together with the pestle. Add the peanuts and pound to a coarse paste. Add the tomatoes and beans and gently mash them. Add the papaya, mango, palm sugar, fish sauce, lime juice, and tamarind water and gently mash with the pestle.

Serve the fish with the rice and papaya salad.

STEAMED FISH

1 to 2 banana leaves (1 large leaf may suffice but 2 is best to be safe)

4 fillets of any fish you like that steams well—I like rockling

4 makrut lime leaves

2 stalks lemongrass, cut in half

Four ¼-inch (6 mm) slices galangal (reserved from the rice on the opposite page)

4 roots from cilantro sprigs

PAPAYA SALAD

4 garlic cloves

Pinch of salt

1 to 4 bird's-eye chilies

2 tablespoons roasted peanuts

6 cherry tomatoes, each cut into eighths

5 snake beans or green beans, cut into ¾-inch (2 cm) pieces

2 cups (350 g) shredded green papaya

1 green mango, peeled, pitted, and shredded

1 tablespoon palm sugar

2 tablespoons fish sauce

1 tablespoon lime juice

1 tablespoon tamarind water

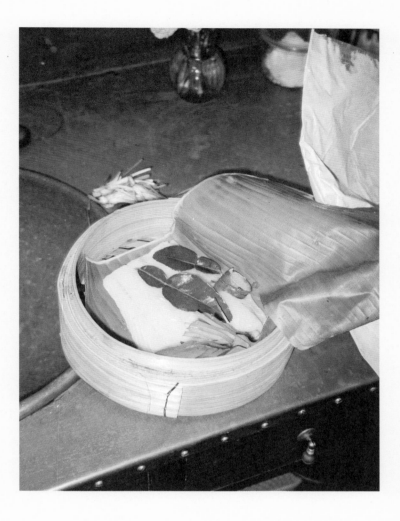

Nicole Wilson

Nicole is a lifelong lover of music who gets to fulfill that passion every day through her job as a music producer. She lives in Portland, Oregon, with her son, Crosby, who is an enthusiastic collector of nature's many treasures.
—

Where does your love of the outdoors come from?
It comes from growing up in Los Angeles and being outdoors easily 50 percent of the time. Playing in the yard as a kid, beach days with friends, summer camps, school campuses that were open-air. It's a part of who I am; it's in my blood.

What in nature brings you joy?
The beach—specifically a beach in California—is my most calm and peaceful place. Since I can't be there regularly now that I live in Portland, I find a lot of joy in stillness and observation—watching the sky change at dusk, listening to birds in our backyard, or letting a warm summer breeze wash over me. The variety and palette of the natural world never cease to amaze me.

How do you define well-being? What tangible daily acts do you practice to claim it for yourself?
For me, it's the opposite of busyness—being present and content with where I'm at. It can be as small as stopping mid-task to hug Crosby, or something more intentional, like an early morning to myself or an evening walk to clear my mind.

How has your relationship with the outdoors affected and informed the way you live in your home?
When I was looking for a house, natural light was one of the most important things to me. I wanted to have a Portland version of the indoor/outdoor living approach that is so natural in Southern California. The summer (and sometimes part of the spring) is my golden season. I'm eating outside, reading and napping there, gardening, and watching my son play in the backyard. I try to spend time outdoors whenever it's not raining, but during the cold, rainy winter months, the big picture windows we put in really become my connection to the outdoors.

What do you find to be the true value of gathering around food with friends?

The deep joy that hospitality brings. The joy of living in the present and letting the conversation just happen. Appreciating and accepting the imperfect is key to a comfortable time with friends and/or family.

What are your favorite rituals around food and eating with others?

Easy, seasonal snacks and a good bottle of wine. And, of course, the right music to help set the vibe. I have playlists of new music, '60s and '70s favorites, and Brazilian jazz that are steadily rotated through.

What kind of food or meal do you most enjoy sitting down to?

I love pasta and often find myself getting the most creative when preparing it—ingredient improvisation! Summer mezze plates are also fun, because they'll often include many things from our garden. I enjoy creating snack boards for my book club friends as well. Eating as many of these meals as possible on our patio table or on a picnic blanket is peak pleasure for me.

How has your heritage influenced the way you think about food and sharing it with others? Or, are there special memories you have around food and/or the outdoors that are tied to your cultural heritage?

My heritage is something I've become more proud of and curious about as I've gotten older. My dad's parents wanted their kids to perfect their English so they would do well in school, versus speaking fluent Spanish, so their Latin heritage was minimized, as in many other families that were trying to assimilate and create a better life for their kids. The one cultural tradition around food that started in my youth and that I've carried through adulthood is tamales at the holidays. Christmas morning doesn't feel like Christmas morning without a breakfast of tamales after we open our gifts. I suppose that my love of cooking and eating outdoors is also culturally influenced. Both my parents were born and raised in Los Angeles, and the ease of grilling and eating outside together was something that started in my dad's youth and carried on throughout my childhood.

What gives you the biggest thrill about working in your garden and growing some of your own food?

The thing I love most about having a small raised-bed veggie garden is tending it with Crosby. As he's gotten older, he understands more about the process and enjoys helping out. It's fun to see him be proud of the cucumbers or Sungolds he grows. I also love a quiet peaceful hour in the morning or evening by myself cleaning up the garden and appreciating the space.

What has Crosby's vigor for life, the outdoors, and nature "treasures" reinvigorated for you?

It takes a big effort for me to see past the clutter of the seventy-sixth "special" rock he's collected or the pile of sticks he adds to weekly, but I'm doing better! I'll empty out his pockets to find pinecones, leaves, flowers, pebbles ("gems"), et cetera, but now it just makes me laugh. His imagination is so pure, and his creative process is such a special thing. I love observing his way of learning about the world around him and how he exists in it. It's a gift to witness his joy of discovery, and I don't want to limit that by telling him he can't collect another "gem." It reminds me of all the times I played in mud as a kid or collected bugs and the fond memories I still have of all the time spent outdoors. I want him to have awe and respect for nature like I do.

What part of, or activity in, the natural world do you find most healing or grounding?

The sound of water. In the past, it's always been watching and listening to waves crash at my favorite beaches in California, but now it has grown to include the sound of a paddleboard cutting through a clear lake, or even falling asleep to the sound of rain. The different sounds water can make are all deeply grounding and calming to me.

—

California Tuna Salad

The perfect quick salad for picnicking anywhere! The recipe is very flexible. If you want to feed more people, add another can of tuna and another half or whole avocado, as well as more nuts and celery; you could also add some canned chickpeas.

SERVES 1 OR 2

One 5-ounce (140 g) can of tuna (I prefer the kind packed in olive oil because then you can use some of that oil for the salad)

1 medium avocado, halved, pitted, and peeled

Salt and pepper

Olive oil (use some from the tuna can, if you like)

1 to 2 celery stalks, cut into ¼-inch (6 mm) slices, or diced if the stalks are wide

⅓ cup (30 g) sliced almonds (or sunflower seeds, pistachios, cashews, or whatever you have on hand)

Any herbs you have on hand (I like chopped chives and fennel fronds, and dill)

Crackers and pickles for serving

Put the tuna and avocado in a medium bowl and mash together with a fork, however chunky or combined you like it. Season with salt and pepper. How well the avocado covers the tuna will determine how much olive oil to add; I usually use 1½ to 2 teaspoons. Add the celery and nuts, stirring gently to combine. Season again with salt, pepper, and/or olive oil to taste if necessary. Add the herbs and stir until just combined.

Serve with crackers or make into a sandwich. Don't forget pickles on the side!

SUMMER IS MY GOLDEN SEASON.

I'm in love with the subtleties in color and texture,
the delight in finding a small otherworldly
natural object from deep in the sea.

—Heidi Joy Baker

GATHERING
AT HOME

Our homes are layered with *us*, wholly reflecting the tiny worlds we create for ourselves. Hosting at home is wonderful for so many reasons. Friends and family get a window into your soul, and there's no need to pack anything up—just grab and go from the kitchen to wherever you're inhaling the fresh air and sunshine (or clouds) together. Gathering in your own space gives you license to call the shots (when, how, what, where) and choose the menu. You can gussy things up or keep it relaxed. You can make do with whatever version of outdoor space you have available, even if it's a cramped concrete patio or a shared city stoop. The point is, having people over is really the ultimate invitation to belonging. Everyone wants to belong somewhere. Why not let them belong at *your* home, with you?

Tina Frey

Tina's home accessories line, TF Design, takes color and fun to a whole new level for every room in the house—and for stress-free outdoor living and dining (her pieces are cast in shatter-resistant resin).
—

What's your relationship with the sun?

I absolutely love a sunny day, particularly when it's paired with nice warm weather! It is hard not to wake up and smile when you see a blue sky. I grew up in Calgary, Alberta, and it was known as "Sunny Alberta" because the province gets so many sunny days a year. Whenever it was sunny out, it meant doing something outside even if it was freezing cold. I grew up with lots of biking, hiking, skiing, canoeing, kayaking, and just being outdoors among the forest and trees. We had superlong days in the summer, and I really enjoyed the abundant daylight then. Living in San Francisco can be a bit rough since it is so often foggy in the summer. I've realized how I truly miss the sunshine and warmth at that time of year and just how important it is to me. Jochen, my husband, and I try to escape as much as possible.

How has your relationship with the outdoors affected and informed the way you live in your home?

Being outdoors and in the sunshine is truly nourishing to the body and mind. I love to be in a space with good natural light, and we don't have many windows with curtains unless it is absolutely necessary for privacy. I love being awakened naturally by the rising sun in the morning, and being able to see the sky is important to bringing that indoors. I don't even need to set an alarm clock, since it is easy to go with the flow of the natural cycles. I also have a lot of plants around the house, and that is another good way to bring the outdoors inside.

What in nature brings you joy?

I appreciate the seasons and their effects on the environment and us. When we are in the rainy season, everything turns an amazing green color as flowers and grasses spring up all over the yard. You can hear the birds singing at dawn and at dusk, and then the frogs start to croak in the early evenings. I love watching the light and how the days get longer in spring and into summer. Then the heat of the summer turns everything a golden yellow, and we appreciate the coolness of the ocean and swimming in it. The long summer evenings are so lovely since they bring relief from the heat of the daytime, and it is so nice to be outdoors into the night. Winters, with their short days, are beautiful in a completely different way, as they make us look forward to the next cycle beginning again.

What are your favorite rituals around food and eating with others?

I love going to the market to see what is in season. I let whatever we find be the inspiration for what we are going to cook. We have a few favorite recipes that can be varied depending on what is freshest at the time, for example, a fruit galette. It works with anything from stone fruit to berries, and it is particularly nice with whipped cream or homemade ice cream on top. This has become the requested dessert if I am asked to make this course of the meal.

What's one significant memory or feeling from your childhood surrounding eating with others?

I was born in Hong Kong, and a typical Chinese meal was shared at a round table with family and friends every weekend. These ranged from simple meals to elaborate multicourse dinners or celebrations, always with many people, with lots of conversation and laughter.

Can you share something about your creative journey and how it has led you to where you are today?

I started my company and second career fourteen years ago. I was not sure how to go about it at first, but I knew I wanted to make things. Despite coming from a background in finance, I did not begin by making a business plan. I knew I had to throw all that out the window, fly by the seat of my pants, and go with my gut. And I knew I wanted to work with a material that had limitless capabilities, would feed my creativity, and had some uniqueness to it. I realized that I owned a lot of books about resin. It is a material that I'd always been fascinated by, and I did lots of reading and experimenting, as well as taking courses on sculpting, mold making, and casting resin. I started out with a couple of samples that

I exhibited at a trade show, and I got some orders and people asking for more designs, and it grew from there.

What part of, or activity in, the natural world do you find most healing or grounding?

I need to be in nature and in the sea or among the trees on a regular basis to stay grounded. Just as we need to sleep, breathe fresh air, and eat healthy food, getting out in nature is simply a necessity, otherwise, we can become very out of touch with ourselves.

When do you find yourself most attuned to nature?

Escaping the city definitely helps. Hiking trails are easily accessible from where I live. I like having the peace and quiet, being able to listen to the birds in the trees and the leaves rustling in the wind, and feeling the warm sun on your face.

—

Seasonal Fruit Galette

This recipe is my own take on Melissa Clark's galette recipe, originally printed in the New York Times. It's my go-to when I need to impress my family and friends since it is super easy. You can use any seasonal fruit that is readily available, and it always tastes delicious. I usually vary the sugar depending on how sweet the fruit is. You can even adapt the recipe to make a savory galette by using onions, tomatoes, or other veggies and cheese if you don't add sugar to the recipe.

SERVES 8

CRUST

1⅓ cups (165 g) all-purpose flour, plus more for working with the dough

1 tablespoon (13 g) sugar

½ teaspoon (3 g) fine sea salt

1 large (50 g) egg

Heavy cream

8 tablespoons (1 stick/113 g) unsalted butter, cut into big pieces

FILLING

3 cups (about 465 g) summer fruit of your choice (such as berries, stone fruit, or figs, sliced or cubed if necessary)

⅓ to ½ cup (65 to 100 g) sugar

Pinch of salt

Grated zest and juice of ½ lemon (optional)

3 to 4 tablespoons (25 to 35 g) cornstarch (if necessary for stone fruit)

¼ cup (40 g) halved or quartered pistachios (optional)

Whipped cream or ice cream for serving (optional)

To make the crust, in a food processor or in a large bowl, pulse or mix together the flour, sugar, and salt. Lightly beat the egg in a measuring cup, then add just enough cream to get to ⅓ cup (80 ml). Lightly whisk the egg and cream together.

Add the butter to the flour, sugar, and sea salt mixture. Work it with your hands to a crumbly consistency and add the egg mixture until you have ¼ cup (60 ml) left. You will be using the remainder of this mixture for the edge of the crust. If using a food processor, do not overprocess; you want a large crumb–like texture. It should start to come together and be like a workable dough ball.

Turn the dough out onto a lightly floured counter and pat it together. The dough performs best if chilled for at least 2 hours, but sometimes I skip this step if I'm in a hurry. If you do chill, make the dough ball into a disc shape, wrap in plastic, and store in the refrigerator for up to 3 days.

Preheat the oven to 400°F (200°C). On a floured surface, roll the dough out to a 12-inch (30 cm) round (it can be ragged, but make sure there are no thin sections in the crust). Transfer to a large rimmed baking sheet lined with parchment paper and chill while you prepare the filling.

To make the filling, in a large bowl, mix together the fruit, sugar to taste (reserving 1 tablespoon for the crust), salt, and lemon zest and juice, if using. Add the cornstarch as needed for juicier fruits (i.e., stone fruit) to ensure it doesn't get runny during baking. You will need less cornstarch for berries.

Pile all the fruit, or neatly arrange slices of stone fruit, on the crust. Leave about a 1-inch (3 cm) border. Gently fold the border over the edge of the fruit all around to keep the fruit and juices from spilling out during baking. You can make this look rustic. If using the pistachios, add them now, sprinkling them evenly over the fruit mixture. Use a pastry brush to brush the remaining egg and heavy cream mixture on the edge of the crust. Sprinkle the remaining sugar on the crust.

Bake the galette for 35 to 45 minutes, until the filling bubbles up and the crust is golden brown. Cool on a wire rack for at least 20 minutes. Serve warm or at room temperature. It's extra delicious served with whipped cream or ice cream. Enjoy!

Maj and Frederik Henriques

This Danish family uprooted themselves from Copenhagen and replanted themselves in Santa Barbara to establish the US branch of Simple Feast—a wildly popular plant-based food delivery service. Maj illuminates the new rhythms and rituals they've adopted since moving to the West Coast.

—

Where does your love of the outdoors come from?
I think that being from Denmark means we're kind of raised to go outdoors whenever we can. Since the weather is so cold and wet there, any time we get the opportunity, we go. In California, that's always possible. In Denmark, you see people eating outdoors wearing big jackets and scarves, and going through a struggle to do it.

What's your relationship with the sun?
Being in the sun means being able to let go. Our bodies don't have to be tense, with our shoulders up to our ears and all bundled up. It's hard to be in a bad mood when the sun is shining. It still feels like such a luxury just to open the door and feel the sun on my face, and the smell of the sun on someone's skin; this is the best, the best.

How would you define well-being, and what kind of practical daily acts do you do to claim that for yourself?
I've started to wake up earlier to have some alone time with my husband, and then we sit in these two chairs in the living room and we light the fire. The sun is just starting to peek out. Having half an hour of calm and the first coffee, that's magical. And then I hike, every day. It's become such an outlet, being in the sun and nature, taking in the smells and feeling my heart pump.

How has your relationship with nature and the outdoors affected and informed the way you live in your home?
One of the first things I do in the morning is open up the windows and doors. I need to feel fresh air, always. I think that's Danish; we're used to having all our windows and doors open even when it's minus degrees. It helps to be in touch. I also take my duvet outside every

morning to freshen it in the sun. In the evening, I love taking it inside again and smelling the sun and the air; everything's fresh and crisp.

What do you find to be the true value of gathering around food with friends?

Food is such a disarming thing. Once you've shared food, you can talk about more serious issues. You don't have to, but when you share a meal, it kind of opens up the channels for communication. That's also why we're strict about eating together as a family. If we're all at home, we eat together. You don't just go into the kitchen and make your own meal. We share our breakfast, we share lunch and dinner, and that's just how it is. We set the table, and we talk. I feel that's a very important structure.

What in nature brings you joy?

Everything about nature brings me joy because it's for all the senses. It's the smells; it's the view. Whenever I'm struggling with something, or my kids are not in a good mood, as soon as we get outside, that all kind of disappears. And you just blend into the natural universe. All the little things don't matter anymore, because you can just enjoy being.

What are some of your favorite rituals around food and eating with others?

As I've gotten older, I've wanted to make it simpler, and not to feel that I have to impress people. I'd rather have people over and order pizza than not have them over because I don't have the energy to make a full meal.

What kind of food or meal do you most enjoy sitting down to?

Plant food. I also love little dishes that you're sharing and that you just keep eating. It's nice to be able to get everything out on the table at once. People sit down and talk, and you're not having to run back and forth. No plating another course. As soon as I've served the food, I can join the party.

What's one significant memory or feeling from your childhood surrounding eating with others?

Being in our summerhouse. It's somewhere you go throughout the summer, and we had just endless summers on the northern coast of the island of Zealand. Everything's about food when you're there—like, what is the next meal going to be? We would set up nets to catch shrimp in the evening, and then in the morning, if there were shrimp in them, someone would prepare them and we would sit down to eat them. I think those are my most specific or clear childhood memories, with very traditional Danish dishes that often take a long time to prepare. These things become part of your routine during the days you're there.

What's one of your favorite meals to make as a family? Or when you have guests over?

It's changing as my kids grow older. I feel so lucky that they eat all kinds of food. But we're all curious about trying new food, and I'm never worried about them not eating it. So I think my favorite meal is more the feeling of having planned something and doing it together and sitting down and seeing everything just come together. And there's all this food in front of you as good as you imagined.

What is one special thing you like to do in nature as a family?

For me, it's hiking. For my family, it's surfing. When they surf, I enjoy sitting on the beach and watching them in the water.

How would you say the natural world has affected your work?

It's totally recalibrating being outdoors. Things fall into place when I'm surrounded by nature.

—

THINGS FALL INTO PLACE WHEN
I'M SURROUNDED BY NATURE.

Roasted Squash with Pesto

This makes a foolproof, delicious side dish (or a light main course) at practically any time of year.

Preheat the oven to 400°F (200°C). Rub any kind of halved squash or pumpkin you like with olive oil, minced garlic, and chopped herbs—whatever fresh herbs you have. Drizzle with a bit of honey and vinegar. Sprinkle with salt and pepper.

Put the squash on a baking sheet and roast until dark and caramelized. Start checking for doneness after 45 minutes. The flesh should be fork-tender. Serve with homemade pesto (recipe follows).

Fresh Herb Pesto

Use any kind of fresh herb you like (but stick to one kind). Put the herbs in a blender, add roasted nuts such as pine nuts or almonds or untoasted walnuts, and blend to a coarse puree. Add chopped garlic or scallions, olive oil, some salt and pepper, and lemon zest to taste and blend well.

Cat Chen

VP of marketing for Amber Interiors, Cat has recently embarked on establishing her own wine label, Dulan (named for the oceanside Taiwanese town where her father lives).
—

Where does your love of the outdoors come from?
I grew up in suburbia, and my family wasn't big on outdoor activities, but when I moved to San Francisco at eighteen years old and discovered the redwood forests just north of the Golden Gate Bridge, I fell in love. I spent a lot of time during those years exploring Northern California and its beauty—the forests, the rivers, the beaches, the vistas. I found a feeling of freedom in so many aspects of my life during that time, and nature was a major part of it.

How do you define well-being? What tangible daily acts do you practice to claim it for yourself?
It's being at peace and being gentle with yourself. It requires being brutally honesty with yourself. I journal throughout the day. Anytime I feel anxious or sad,

I quickly jot it down. Then I immediately release that feeling.

What do you find to be the true value of gathering around food with friends?
The conversation, the laughter, the joy. It quite literally feeds the soul. It's nourishing and comforting.

What are your favorite rituals around food and eating with others?
Preparing the food and the space with intention, and with the specific person in mind. Cooking is my meditation. I get into a Zen-like state. I have had some of my best epiphanies then. It's soothing and calming. But the most enjoyable part to me is sharing the food and watching someone take that first bite. There's nothing that brings me more joy than nourishing my friends and family.

What's one significant memory or feeling from your childhood connected to eating with others?
I grew up in a big Taiwanese family. Every weekend, our entire family would gather in a cul-de-sac, where my

grandmother, aunts, and uncles lived next door to each other. My brother, cousins, and I would play together outside, and the adults would be cooking inside. By sunset, we'd all come into the house to eat the best homemade Taiwanese food. The nights would end with my mom, aunts, and grandmother playing mah-jongg while snacking on pistachios. I wish I could do it all over again. I'll never forget those moments.

What place in nature have you found offers you the most profound rest and restoration?
My father's home in Dulan, Taiwan. It's in a small village, and the house sits at the base of Dulan Mountain, which is covered in trees and only a mile (1.5 km) from the Pacific Ocean. It's a simple place, surrounded by shades of green and blue, with cows grazing the fields, monkeys in the trees, and the sound of birds. It's a tropical paradise where you eat locally grown vegetables and fresh-caught fish. It's as beautiful as it is delicious in Dulan.

What's your favorite scent in nature that immediately transports you to a different time and/or place?
The smell of the salty ocean air and the feeling of it on my skin and hair is my favorite. I could stare at the horizon for days.

—

Mama Alice's Pork and Shrimp Dumplings

I love to make these dumplings for special occasions with friends or family—especially when I'm hosting in my own backyard!

NOTE: Think of the measurements in this recipe as basic guidelines. The proportions of most of the ingredients can be changed according to your own preferences!

SERVES 8

FILLING

1 pound (455 g) ground pork

8 ounces (225 g) shrimp, peeled and cut into small pieces

1 large (50 g) egg

2 cups (140 g) finely chopped cabbage

3 scallions, finely chopped

1 tablespoon soy sauce

1 tablespoon toasted sesame oil

1 package round dumpling wrappers (I don't make them from scratch!)

SAUCE

¼ cup (55 g) thinly sliced scallions

¼ cup (35 g) minced garlic

½ cup (120 ml) soy sauce (or more, to cover the scallions and garlic)

White vinegar

Asian sesame oil

2 tablespoons sugar

To make the filling, combine the pork, shrimp, egg, cabbage, scallions, soy sauce, and sesame oil in a bowl and mix together with your hands.

Set a small bowl of water to the side of your work surface. Place a small spoonful of the filling in the center of a dumpling wrapper. Dip your finger in the bowl of water and wet the edges of one half of the wrapper. Fold the wrapper over to enclose the filling and pinch the edges together to seal. Repeat with the remaining filling and more dumpling wrappers. Set aside.

To make the sauce, fill a jar with the scallions and minced garlic. Add enough soy sauce to cover the scallions and garlic, then add a few splashes each of the vinegar and sesame oil. Add the sugar and stir. Let the sauce sit until the sugar dissolves. (The sauce can be made up to 1 day in advance and stored in the refrigerator.)

To cook the dumplings, bring a large pot of water to a boil. Working in batches to avoid crowding the pot, add the dumplings to the boiling water. Once the water returns to a boil, add a cup (240 ml) of cold water and let the water come to a boil once again. When the dumplings float to the top, after 5 to 7 minutes, they should be done. Remove the dumplings with a slotted spoon and place in a bowl.

Serve the dumplings with the sauce.

Things to Ponder on a Sunny Day

Sometimes you just need to let your mind wander and see where it takes you. These are easy prompts for getting started.

~ Imagine your childhood home or any other place you loved as a kid. Walk through the rooms in your mind, and then step outside. Look through the hedges, or sit beneath the trees. Where did you feel safest?

~ When was the last time you really played? How would you like to invite play into your life again?

~ What are you noticing in your life? What are you actively *not* noticing?

~ Are you breathing deeply?

~ In which areas of your life could you calm down?

~ What were some rituals your family had around gathering when you were growing up? Have you maintained any of these as you've gotten older?

~ Who in your life gets you to think most deeply about the way things are? Who in turn do you help process life?

~ What's your favorite kind of magical thinking?

~ When was the last time you had a profound moment in nature?

~ Have you left space in your life for spontaneity?

Lana and Darrick Rasmussen

Lana and Darrick are craftspeople—primarily working with paper or wood, respectively—who live in the Valley of the Moon (also known as Ojai, California), with their son, Bay. Lana gives us a picture of their current days under the sun, along with insight into her own upbringing.

—

Where does your love of the outdoors come from?

I had the great fortune of growing up near the sea and being able to travel the greater part of the West for weeks at a time with my family. The Pacific Ocean was the cultural anchor in my hometown, particularly because of the ubiquitous influence of surfing. Although surf culture felt more like an exclusive boys' club in my youth, I developed my own relationship with the water early on. To know the ocean is to be humbled by it. I feel like that idea carried through to all of my experiences with soil, mountains, rivers, rocks, and lakes, as well as, of course, fresh food.

What's your relationship with the sun?

I love the reliability of the sun. I've found that recently all I want to do is draw the sun. One project in the queue is a grid of sun drawings, more as an exercise. Years ago, I worked for a land artist who created works using the sun and sky of New Mexico as his medium. I've never been the same since.

How do you define well-being? What tangible daily acts do you practice to claim it for yourself?

In short, prioritizing my body and play is what keeps me feeling well and keeps me from taking myself too seriously. There's such a grand recalibration that you're faced with weekly and even daily as a working mother and creative artist. One must stay limber in all ways! Keeping my body strong and stretched is the best thing I can do for myself, my people, and my work. I'd characterize play as participating in an activity that requires some form of improvisation (and, if I'm lucky, a little discomfort), such as dancing like a fool with my son, freehand drawing, crafting functionless creatures, experimenting in the garden, or rearranging my living

space. And let's not discount the healing properties of dark chocolate.

How has your relationship with the outdoors affected and informed the way you live in your home?

We've just moved into a light-filled house that accentuates what's happening in the garden. I am so inspired by food forests and the idea of creating pockets of discovery within a garden that appeal to all of the senses.

What do you find to be the true value of gathering around food with friends?

Food is one of life's greatest pleasures. In our climate, we have the luxury of access to freshly grown food year-round. The wealthiest I've ever felt is sitting down to a rustic meal with a group of farmers. (They know how to party!) With the best ingredients, all you really need are fat and seasoning. No fuss. But absolutely the most important part is to enjoy every single bite. I tell my son this all the time.

What are your favorite rituals around food and eating with others?

A dear friend recently took another friend and me to her orchard to pick mulberries. She made us blush with the verbal warning that this was going to be a very "sensual experience." Indeed, it was quite the scene, the three of us covered in mulberry juice, giggling. We'll be making this a tradition.

What kind of food or meal do you most enjoy sitting down to?

With good company, I'm pretty easy to please. I enjoy the entire spectrum, from fine dining to camp-stove meals. Food culture is infinitely fascinating. In the words of Anthony Bourdain, "Food is everything we are."

What's one significant memory or feeling from your childhood surrounding eating with others?

My aunt Yvonne lived on a big rural property in Auburn, California. Whenever we visited her, she'd wake up hours before the rest of us and collect fresh eggs from the coop, whip up multiple pastries using homemade jam, and put out all the cereal boxes with milk, yogurt, coffee, tea, and fruit juice. When I woke up at her house, I felt like Kevin from *Home Alone 2* getting room service at the Plaza. I truly felt the essence of abundance and love in her heart.

Growing up in Southern California and living here most of your life, what have you found that you uniquely appreciate about nature and the seasons here? Is there anything you feel that you've missed out on?

I lived on the East Coast in my twenties. And Darrick and I lived together for a couple of years in a much wetter climate in Northern California, which we miss a lot. You truly do have to leave Southern California to understand seasons. But here the year-round growing season is the gift!

What I do miss about a more defined seasonal shift is the natural rhythm to retreat in the winter and then to return to camaraderie in the community when things warm up. For example, when that very first sparkle of spring presents itself, there's such a celebratory electricity in the air.

What do you love most about living in Ojai?

With the unique east-to-west orientation of the valley, I'd argue that Ojai catches one of the best Alpenglow sunsets in the world. Orange blossoms explode in the east end. People walk their goats and ponies among the grand oaks in the neighborhoods. Local artists collaborate in myriad ways. Due to fierce resistance against development in Ojai, land conservation efforts, and local pride, this has remained a very rural setting. We all know we have something special here, which is why people are so quick to claim it as their own (for better or worse). Every year, Ojai is threatened by wildfires, so I try to maintain perspective about the land we're so lucky to share here.

—

Spring Radicchio-Citrus Salad

A bright and versatile salad for any summer gathering.

SERVES 4

DRESSING

¼ cup (60 ml) fresh grapefruit juice

6 tablespoons (90 ml) extra-virgin olive oil

Salt and pepper

SALAD

1 head red radicchio or Treviso radicchio

3 tangerines, peeled and separated into segments

2 avocados, halved, pitted, and sliced into thick chunks

2 shallots, thinly sliced

1 cup (110 g) Parmesan shavings (cut from a chunk of cheese with a vegetable peeler)

A large handful of basil leaves, torn into small pieces

To make the dressing, whisk together the grapefruit juice, olive oil, and salt and pepper to taste in a small bowl.

To make the salad, cut or tear the radicchio crosswise into 1-inch-wide (3 cm) strips. Combine the radicchio, tangerines, avocado, shallots, Parmesan shavings, and basil in a medium bowl and toss gently.

To serve, drizzle the dressing over the salad and enjoy.

Sandra Adu-Zelli

Originally from the UK, Sandra now lives on the West Coast, where she owns and runs Gipsy Hill Bakery, a pop-up heavily influenced by and reliant upon the year-round Santa Barbara farmers' market.

—

How do you define well-being? What tangible daily acts do you practice to claim it for yourself?
Well-being to me is being in sound mind and spirit. Surrounding myself with people who fill my bucket, not deplete it. Taking time to check in with myself, to notice how I'm feeling. Trying to be present in my world.

What do you find to be the true value of gathering around food with friends?
I love nothing more than to be around a table eating delicious food and drinking good wine while chatting and laughing with great people. It's the connection, the excitement, and the anticipation of the next course, whether it be at a restaurant or at home with family.

What brings you joy in nature?
Walking on the beach. Growing up, I lived on the east coast of England, and we always went to the beach in the summer. The North Sea is not quite the same as Santa Barbara—thankfully! Living here, I have come to really appreciate the beautiful beach walks. I always feel 100 percent better after a beach walk, but I don't do it enough!

What kind of food or meal do you most enjoy sitting down to?
Growing up British, having Ghanaian parents, training in classic French cuisine, and marrying an Italian make for a very diverse culinary background. I trained in London, which is a huge melting pot of cultures and cuisines. All of those cuisines are equally delicious to me. However, today I might crave Indian food; I find it so comforting and soothing, especially the dals, with naan bread. Tomorrow it might be a West African dish of jollof rice with a rich, spicy stew, or even pizza. The experience I most enjoy is any time I get to be convivial with others.

What's one significant memory or feeling from your childhood surrounding eating with others?
Eating Ghanaian food with my family, learning the names of new dishes, tasting different types of food—so different from the English experience and range of foods.

How has the landscape of Santa Barbara affected you, your work, and the way you interact with the outdoors?
My kids were born here, and through them, I've gotten to experience the outdoors in ways that I might not have done before I had them. Making the time to be out in nature, especially walking on the beach, is always a tonic. Twice-weekly trips to our fabulous farmers' market have brought much-loved and valued friendships and culinary experiences that I cherish.

What keeps you down-to-earth and grounded? What puts you off-balance?
Grounded: landscapes, lush green fields, the beach. Off-balance: the destruction of nature, the climate emergency!

What's your favorite scent in nature that immediately transports you to a different time and place?
The heady scent of jasmine in the early evenings in spring . . . it takes me back to being in Thailand with my husband.

What makes you feel most like yourself?
Being in a professional kitchen. Being part of a team. As soon as I walk in and tie on my apron, I just feel completely myself; my only responsibility is to prep, cook, and do my very best.

—

Corn and Shishito Pepper Flatbread

A delicious addition to any get-together, for eating at home or on the go.

MAKES 8 FLATBREADS

DOUGH

2 cups (260 g) bread flour, plus more for working with the dough

1¾ teaspoons (7 g) active dry yeast

1½ teaspoons (7 g) baking powder

1¼ teaspoons (8 g) sea salt

¾ cup (180 ml) lukewarm water

About 1½ tablespoons olive oil

TOPPING

2 cups (290 g) corn kernels

2 cups (300 g) shishito peppers

¼ cup (10 g) coarsely chopped cilantro, plus more for garnish

¼ cup (15 g) thinly sliced scallions

4 to 5 tablespoons (60 to 75 ml) olive oil

Juice of 1 lime

Salt and pepper

1 tablespoon Calabrian chili paste or other chili paste, such as sambal oelek

2 limes cut into 8 wedges

SPECIAL EQUIPMENT

Pizza stone

To make the dough, combine the flour, yeast, baking powder, and salt in the bowl of a stand mixer fitted with the paddle attachment and mix on low speed for about 30 seconds. Add the lukewarm water and mix until you have a rough dough. Allow the dough to rest for 5 minutes.

Turn on the mixer and knead the dough for 3 to 5 minutes, until you have a smooth dough. Generously oil a large bowl, place the dough in the bowl, and cover with a clean tea towel. Let rest in a draft-free area for 30 minutes.

Place a pizza stone on the lower oven rack and preheat the oven to 500°F (260°C).

While the dough is resting, make the topping: Heat a large cast-iron skillet over medium heat until very hot. Add the corn and cook, without stirring, for 2 minutes, then stir quickly and cook for 1 to 2 minutes longer, until the corn is lightly charred. Transfer the corn to a medium bowl.

Wipe out the skillet and heat again until very hot. Add the shishitos and dry-roast, turning occasionally, until the skin is evenly blistered all over. Remove from the heat.

Stir the cilantro and scallions into the bowl with the corn. Add 1 to 2 tablespoons of the olive oil and the lime juice and mix well. Add salt and pepper to taste. Set aside.

In a small bowl, mix the chili paste or flakes with the remaining 3 tablespoons of olive oil. Let sit while you make the flatbread.

Divide the dough into 8 equal pieces and roll each one into a ball. Let rest for 5 minutes.

On a floured countertop, using a floured rolling pin, roll each ball into 5- to 6-inch (13 to 15 cm) rounds about ¼ inch (6 mm) thick. Place on a baking sheet.

Top the rounds with the corn mix, dividing it equally. Place the shishito peppers on top of the corn.

Place on the hot pizza stone and bake for 5 to 8 minutes, until golden brown in color. Remove from the oven, transfer the flatbreads to a cooling rack, and let cool for 5 minutes.

To serve, drizzle the flatbreads with the chili oil and garnish with chopped cilantro and the lime wedges.

Heidi Joy Baker

Heidi's clothing line, Ozma of California, has been redefining what casual comfort, natural beauty, and feeling good in one's own skin should look like since its creation in 2015.

—

Where does your love of the outdoors come from?
My love of the outdoors was born from being a really lucky kid who took so much of my experience growing up for granted—and often being a bit of a brat about it! I grew up with super-outdoorsy and environmentally conscious parents who loved taking me and my brother hiking, camping, exploring national parks, all of that good stuff. I remember hating the bugs and the heavy backpacks.

When I was eight or so, I realized that where my heart really lay in nature was in the water! My folks sent me to summer camp on a tiny lake in Vermont, and I absolutely came alive when I discovered that I could spend *all* of my time sitting on the dock, swimming, canoeing, or sailing. I felt so free! (Also, drifting in the breeze on the water was way more appealing than being in hot hiking boots and smothered in bug spray.) I became smitten with sailing the camp's little Sunfish sailboats. The way the water moved, the thrill of that small vessel heeling to its edge, the fun of jumping off the side of the boat and taking turns being dragged behind it. I barely left the glassiness of that lake till I was too old to be a camper.

What's your relationship with the sun?
The feeling of the sun warming my skin always immediately lowers my blood pressure.

How do you define well-being? What tangible daily acts do you practice to claim it for yourself?
I somewhat redefine this quite often, but it's always about checking in and being honest with myself about what I need. It really boils down to finding an ease in my body and heart so that while not everything in the world is ideal, I'm enjoying pleasure and purpose and love in my everyday life. It's incredibly important for me to get moving outside every morning. Letting my body breathe and my skin feel the fresh air is an instant miracle drug and an irreplaceable reset button.

How has your relationship with the outdoors affected and informed the way you live in your home?

Because I'm living in Los Angeles, the dream of ocean breezes, total privacy, and open nature right out my front window is not exactly my reality right now. Those things are super important for my headspace, so creating my own outdoor oasis within the city has had to be second best. With help from a very talented friend, my partner, Dustin, and I transformed our backyard from a wild and run-down space to a beautifully planned native and drought-tolerant garden, where we can have our own slice of nature. It means peace and quiet without getting into a car. Our friend created different areas for gardening, entertaining, and relaxing, and even for working at home. We are lucky enough to have already had some mature trees, and we planted a bunch of pollinators in the yard, so even though those plants are still tiny, it already feels like we are bringing more nature to us! Hearing tons of birds and watching hummingbirds is so special. First thing in the morning, I walk outside with my coffee and poke around in our veggie beds, check on the plants, and clean dead leaves out of the small branches. Having your hands in dirt is so meditative! The cherry on top is being able to do it in my pajamas.

What do you find to be the true value of gathering around food with friends?

Guaranteed laughs! I've always loved hosting friends— very informal gatherings where everyone contributes food are my favorite. It's all about no stress, joking around, feeling all of the good feels with people you like.

Where is the most pleasure for you in food? Growing it? Preparing it? Sharing it with others?

All of the above! Using ingredients from my garden is super rewarding for me, even if that just means a small bit of herbs or a few leaves of salad. Walking barefoot with a pair of scissors to clip off just enough chives or pinching the tops of the basil or whatever it is that I need is always fun. I love the act of standing at the kitchen counter and prepping a meal with someone I love. There is just so much quality in that together time and the tactile acts of chopping and rinsing, the

creativity in improvisation as things come together. It's all about beautiful ingredients, nice wine, and good company.

What kind of food or meal do you most enjoy sitting down to?

I really enjoy active meals like a build-your-own-sushi-hand-roll party, shabu-shabu, or a many-course tapas-style barbecue. Lots of options and sauces and variations so you get to play with your food as you eat it.

What part of, or activity in, the natural world do you find most healing or grounding?

Surfing! Each and every time I begin to paddle out into the water, there is this amazing weightless, free feeling unlike any other. The moments before and after riding a wave have healing and meditative properties. Seeing dolphins play nearby, watching the color of the sky change just before sunset, or catching up with friends without distraction—all pretty good stuff.

Your home is filled with the most incredible objects found in nature. Have you always been someone who noticed and valued these kinds of easily overlooked treasures?

Well, I'm glad that I haven't kept every rock or shell, but I'm very glad that my collection of heart-shaped coral has made it through several moves. I've always been smitten by nature's beauty. I'm in love with the subtleties in color and texture, the delight in finding a small otherworldly natural object from deep in the sea.

—

Frances Palmer

Frances is a renowned potter who has developed the perfect symbiosis between vessel making and flower growing—her vases inspire the bouquets from her gardens, and her flowers in the garden inspire ever-new forms on the wheel.

—

Where does your love of the outdoors come from?
I grew up in Morristown, New Jersey, which was beautiful and rural at that time. I was able to roam outdoors, and I spent a lot of time perched in our magnolia tree, making up stories.

How do you define well-being? What tangible daily acts do you practice to claim it for yourself?
Well-being is having time to think, be alone, and work at what I love. To listen to myself and follow through with those directions. I take a walk nearly every day, and I work in the garden from March to December. During the winter months, I'm in the greenhouse.

How has your relationship with the outdoors affected and informed the way you live in your home?
I try to keep my interiors simple and filled with flowers. Lots of views to the outside, and potted blooms during the cold months.

What do you find to be the true value of gathering around food with friends?
Nothing expresses love for me better than preparing a meal for friends and family to enjoy together.

What in nature brings you joy?
Observing the miracle of flowers and their geometry.

What are your favorite rituals around food and eating with others?
Baking a splendid cake or concocting a salad from a nearby farm's bounty.

Tessa Tran and Zach Schau

This couple lives on a Mount Washington hillside in northeast LA, where Zach is in commercial real estate and Tessa is CEO and creative director of the jewelry and homewares brand Chan Luu. Zach and Tessa love to grow food, cook, and host friends at their expansive backyard table overlooking the Verdugo Mountains. Tessa illuminates how they invite nature into the everyday, despite living in the city.

—

Where does your love of the outdoors come from?
Zach and I were both born and raised in Los Angeles. With LA's mild seasons, we're lucky enough to be able to spend most of our weekends and other time off outdoors.

What's your relationship with the sun?
Many people love the change in seasons, but we would be totally content if every day were warm and sunny. The fewer clothes, the better, and dining al fresco is always preferable.

How do you define well-being? What tangible daily acts do you practice to claim it for yourself?
Well-being for me is being at peace with myself. There are many ways I claim this, through the work that I do with my community and artisans around the world, through relationships I've nurtured, and by escaping from the daily grind to feel reenergized and inspired.

How has your relationship with the outdoors affected and informed the way you live in your home?
All the work we've done to the house revolves around our outdoor space. Recently we cleaned up a dead space at the back of our house to create a place where we could dine and enjoy the neon sunsets. Zach picked up woodworking so we could design and make our own outdoor furniture, and I expanded our garden, terracing the hill where we've created a food forest.

Katherine Herridge

Katherine hails from Essex, England, and now lives in London with her husband, Nick, and their cat, parrotlet, and school of medaka fish. She manages a grocery shop in the Peckham neighborhood called General Store.

Where does your love of the outdoors come from?
I grew up by the Thames Estuary. The landscape is flat, muted, and gray. The skies are big and unceasing as they are reflected in the flooded salt marshes. We lived by a creek decked with pear trees and hedgerows. I remember catching a stickleback and bringing it to school with me in a jar, and my cat catching a slowworm that I nursed back to health in my dad's seed propagator. Letting snails crawl over my face. Wading out in the estuary mud when the tide went out. Jumping over cowpats. Pushing hay bales down the hill. Spitting on dock leaves to cure nettle stings. Bats flying in through open windows on hot summer nights.

Sunlight and warmth aren't always abundant in the UK. How do you bring nature into your home for the times when it's less pleasant to be outside?
My home is almost overrun with natural objects that I pick up when I'm out and about: shells, rocks, bones, skulls, fallen butterflies, oak galls, acorns, branches, dried-out seaweed, mermaid's purses, and sea urchins. I buy fresh flowers every week. I work in a grocery shop that focuses on seasonal produce, so I always have a bowl on my kitchen counter full of whatever fruit and vegetables are at their best.

How do you define well-being? What tangible daily acts do you practice to claim it for yourself?
Well-being to me means feelings of happiness and comfort. I spend time with my pet bird. I walk to find branches and food to decorate his cage. I feed my medaka fish, which I hatched from eggs. I sit with my cat. I think about dinner. I wear pajamas.

What in nature brings you joy?

The seasons, and the produce that comes with them; plants and creatures.

What is your favorite dish/meal for a spontaneous picnic or garden dinner at home?

Fritti; sandwiches; take-out pizza; barbecued seafood.

Where or how do you feel most fully, freely yourself?

Swimming in the sea.

What regular rhythms bring you peace?

Coffee and Oscar Peterson (a jazz pianist) on weekend mornings. Watching the tide come in and go out again. Preening my parrot. Watering the garden.

Simple Dressing with Game Birds and Squash

This recipe has just a few ingredients and is used to dress both the birds and the squash. It works well on the barbecue, but you could also roast it in a hot oven. I like to cook this dish in the last few days of summer just as the early evenings begin to get darker and colder and you find yourself having to nip indoors to grab sweaters and blankets to keep everyone warm, and candles and lamps so you can see one another.

SERVES 4

DRESSING

5 or more garlic cloves

Agrodolce or other sweet vinegar

Olive oil

3 pinches of chili flakes (I use smoked Greek chili flakes from Daphnis and Chloe)

2 pinches of salt

2 or 3 game birds (partridges or pheasants) or 1 whole chicken, spatchcocked

1 squash (delicata, acorn, or crown), gutted and sliced into ½- to ¾-inch-wide (1 to 2 cm) wedges

Barbecued Cavolo Nero, Parmesan, and Pine Nuts (recipe follows) for serving

Light a charcoal barbecue and let the flames die down while you dress the birds. Or if you're using an oven, preheat to 430°F/(220°C).

To make the dressing, grate the garlic into a jug or bowl. Add a little agrodolce, a generous amount of olive oil, the chili flakes, and the salt and mix well.

Place the birds and sliced squash on two separate baking trays.

Pour half of the dressing over the birds and the remainder over the squash slices. Mix the contents of each tray well to make sure that everything is coated.

Take the spatchcocked birds from their tray and barbecue over a not-too-fierce heat for around half an hour. I use a thermometer to check when they are done; the birds are cooked when an internal temperature reaches 165°F (75°C).

Add the squash slices to the barbecue, cooking until they have nice color and have softened, about 15 minutes. Serve with the Barbecued Cavolo Nero, Parmesan, and Pine Nuts.

Barbecued Cavolo Nero, Parmesan, and Pine Nuts

SERVES 4

Cover some cavolo nero leaves with olive oil and quickly cook on the barbecue so that the leaves have just started to blacken in places.

Put a handful of pine nuts on a square of foil, pinching the sides of the foil inward to make a boat. Cook the pine nuts on a hot barbecue for 1 to 2 minutes, or until brown.

Using the jug from the dressing above if you haven't washed it already, make a dressing: Grate in some Parmesan and add some olive oil and 3 pinches of salt.

To serve, slice the charred cavolo nero leaves and place on a plate. Add the pine nuts and dressing. Finish with some grated Parmesan.

The dawn of each day restores my soul.

—Catherine Welch

GATHERING IN OPEN SPACES

Isn't it just the warmest, most communal feeling when we gather in an open space—a park, a field, a public garden—and find others around us doing the same? There's a hum of festivity buzzing through the air, making whatever kind of occasion you're having, whether calm and quiet or celebratory and boisterous, feel that much more convivial. Or maybe you're the only ones in an open expanse and you're joined by the unsilent silence of nature: birds, cicadas, quivering grasses. Perhaps the distant city sounds. Either way, win-win.

Everyone has access to some sort of open space. It's the most democratic of places to plan a to-do. People sit or lie or lounge on the ground together in the same uniting fashion. There is much to be said for occasionally leaving the table behind. There's something elemental about getting right down on the earth, and you feel it in your body and your senses in a different way. I love seeing a group of all ages scattered haphazardly across the ground (though there's no shame in bringing camp chairs for the creakiest in the bunch). Open spaces can comfort and envelop us in ways that are just as lovely as intimate ones, sometimes for altogether different reasons: the people, the light, the sounds, the vantage point. You really can't go wrong wherever you land.

Ayda Robana

As a private catering chef and food stylist, Ayda brings fragrant North African flavors and dishes full of love to the table whenever she cooks—and people know to never miss a party when Ayda's at the helm. Ayda shares a snapshot of her life in Santa Barbara with her husband, Rick, and their daughter, Lulu.

—

Where does your love of the outdoors come from?
I grew up in a small town in upstate New York, surrounded by nature. I spent countless hours exploring and playing outdoors with friends in a peaceful, beautiful natural environment.

What's your favorite scent in nature that immediately transports you to a different time and place?
First, the scent of decaying leaves. The smell always reminds me of my idyllic childhood. My dad would rake the leaves into piles, and my brother and I would jump into those enormous mounds for hours. Second, the smell of apples in the fall; this reminds me of the years I spent living in southern Vermont.

How do you define well-being? What tangible daily acts do you practice to claim it for yourself?
Being happy and healthy. I surround myself with friends and family I love dearly. Cooking healthy, nutritious food for both loved ones and my clients is my practice of connecting with my heart's work in feeding others.

How has your relationship with the outdoors affected and informed the way you live in your home?
Most of our meals and entertaining take place outdoors at our home. Our outdoor dining area features a table and benches made from a redwood tree that grew in our yard.

What in nature brings you joy?
I find endless joy in nature, particularly in the bounty of food that comes from the land and sea. Walking on the beach brings me joy. Seeing the flowers blooming on Figueroa Mountain in springtime. Skiing. Going for walks in the redwood forests.

Harissa-Roasted Carrot Hummus

SERVES 6 TO 8

5 large or 7 small carrots

¾ cup (180 ml) olive oil

2 garlic cloves, minced

½ teaspoon cumin seeds

½ teaspoon coriander seeds

½ teaspoon nigella seeds

½ teaspoon berbere spice blend

Rind of ½ preserved lemon

1 tablespoon lemon juice

⅓ cup (80 ml) tahini

1 tablespoon jarred harissa
(if using harissa powder or harissa
from a tube, you will need less)

2 tablespoons water

Crudités for serving
(use your favorite raw vegetables)

Cut the carrots into thirds. Bring a large pot of water to a boil, add the carrots, and cook for 15 minutes, or until tender when pierced with a fork. Drain and blot dry with paper towels.

Preheat the oven to 400°F (200°C). Put the carrots on a rimmed baking sheet and toss with ¼ cup (60 ml) of the olive oil, the garlic, and the seeds and spice blend to coat. Roast for 30 minutes, or until caramelized and golden. Remove from the oven and allow to cool.

Combine the preserved lemon, lemon juice, tahini, harissa, water, and cooled carrots in a food processor and process to a puree. With the motor running, drizzle in the remaining ½ cup (120 ml) olive oil and process until smooth. Serve with crudités.

IDEAL SNACKS *for*
EASY GET-TOGETHERS

No need to pull out all the stops for every gathering. Make things easy on yourself and consider this a back-pocket list to choose from for any old shebang.

- SLICED CITRUS
- CASTELVETRANO OLIVES AND WINE
- A POPCORN MEDLEY
- CHOCOLATE, DATES, AND NUTS
- CUBED MELON DRIZZLED WITH LIME JUICE
- LEMON OLIVE OIL CAKE
- PERFECTLY RIPE FIGS
- A GOOD LOAF OF BREAD AND SALTY BUTTER
- CHEESE, CRACKERS, SALAMI, AND JAM
- A PAN OF BROWNIES (NEVER UNDERESTIMATE A GOOD BROWNIE)
- CHIPS, SALSA, AND GUACAMOLE
- GRILLED, SLICED SAUSAGE WITH MUSTARD
- FRESH, CRISP VEGGIES AND HUMMUS
- PASTRIES FROM YOUR FAVORITE BAKERY

What are your favorite rituals around food and eating with others?

When we have guests over or when we're really doing it up with just our family, I always want three courses. You've got to have that salty, crunchy thing with your sparkly cold drink before dinner, then sit down together for the meal, and then take dessert somewhere outside. It's nice to really draw out the whole event.

What kind of food or meal do you most enjoy sitting down to?

I like meals with lots of sauces and toppers. I love to have tons of little bowls to pass around and have everyone build their plate the way they like.

What kind of landscape inspires your freest, most intuitive self?

A cold Texas river lined with cypress trees.

Do you have any habits or routines around spending time in nature that make you feel especially grounded and at peace?

Swimming in natural water and lying down in tall grass, just listening.

Has having children reinspired a sense of play in your life?

The never-ending, always-abounding energy my kids have has for sure reinspired a sense of play in me. It is the only way to survive with them. I play with them, but what I find most joy in is watching them find their own play.

Where are you finding the most vibrant sense of community at this stage of your life?

When we moved, we left all of our close friends and most of our family. We had been within a ten-minute walk of all the people we loved. Leaving that behind has been a huge loss, and that is not something you can rebuild quickly. So right now we are enjoying a smaller community with the four of us, and Ben's parents, and are excited about this stage of making new friends. The people in Fredericksburg have been overwhelmingly welcoming and kind, so we are hopeful that it is only a matter of time until we find our larger community.

Your design work seems so delicately and beautifully influenced by nature and the outside world. How would you describe nature's impact on your design process?

It's not an overly conscious thing. It's just the lens I see through. It has to feel natural in some way for me to relate to it. I don't mean only colors or materials, but also balance and function. It has to all fall into place in just the right way, just the way nature does.

What's your long-term vision for Contigo Ranch and your hopes for the kind of place it can be for people who spend time there?

There are a few goals guiding our decisions at Contigo Ranch, for the land itself and for the people who come to enjoy it. For our guests, we hope a stay on our land will be a time of healing and connection. We believe that the life-giving bond between humans and nature is being strained and broken by our current culture. We hope to provide the space and clarity of mind for people to reconnect with what makes us human—gathering around a fire at night, watching the stars, sitting still to see the sun come up. It is very simple stuff, and that is exactly what we are trying to protect. Our goal with the land is to foster healing and regeneration through sustainable ranching practices. Cultivating a diversity of native plants and animals and creating healthy ecosystems are at the core of this effort.

As a creative practice, the shift from creating spaces for clients to working with my family and nature to bring long-term value to our community and the land is a dream come true. Thinking about how to create beauty for our guests in a way that brings them peace, healing, and connection is exactly where I want to be.

—

Zucchini Dill Pasta

This is the perfect dish for a picnic meal as it can be served warm or cold—both equally delicious.

SERVES 4

Salt

Olive oil

½ sweet onion, diced

Red pepper flakes

4 garlic cloves, chopped

5 medium zucchini, coarsely grated

One 12-ounce (340 g) package fettuccine

½ cup (120 ml) white wine

Grated zest and juice of 2 lemons

A handful of chopped dill, plus more for garnish

A small handful of chopped mint

¼ to ½ cup (30 to 55 g) crumbled feta cheese for serving

Chopped toasted pecans or other nuts of your choice (pistachios would be good) for garnish

Bring a large pot of salted water to a boil.

Meanwhile, heat 2 tablespoons olive oil in a large sauté pan over medium-high heat. Add the onion and cook until translucent. Add salt to taste, a pinch of red pepper flakes, and the garlic and cook until the garlic is fragrant. Add the zucchini and cook until most of the water it releases has evaporated and it is beginning to stick to the pan.

While the zucchini cooks, add the fettuccine to the boiling water and cook until al dente. Drain, reserving 1 cup (240 ml) of the pasta water.

Add the wine to the zucchini and cook until it has evaporated. Add the lemon zest and half the lemon juice. Then add the dill, mint, more olive oil, and salt to taste. The sauce should have a loose-ish consistency; if necessary, add some of the reserved pasta water. Add the fettuccine and toss and stir to mix. If necessary, add salt to taste.

Serve the pasta in bowls, topped with more dill, the feta, and chopped nuts, and finish with a drizzle of the remaining lemon juice.

I THINK THE SUN BURIED
ITSELF IN MY BONES.

The true value of gathering around food
with friends is to slow down and connect. It is
an act of communion. I like small gatherings for
this reason—more intimacy, more connection.

—Kate McMahon

GATHERING
IN INTIMATE SPACES

When we live in a small space, it's easy to think we don't have room to invite people over. But actually, people love intimate spaces. Think of the kitchen at any get-together in recent history. The kitchen is where people always gravitate to, because of the communal, lively feeling of preparing something together—even if you're keeping your host company by drinking a glass of wine or helping to toss the salad. Intimate spaces are where you lower your voices and share your secrets with those you love.

Same goes for gathering outside. Intimate gathering places can be harder to come by when out in the open, but there are a couple of general principles to keep in mind. Pick a place where you feel protected—hidden within the trees, against a cliffside, on top of a big rock. Have a focal point like a picnic blanket, a view, or the feast itself. Or just make do with what you have. The point isn't perfection or prettiness— it's just to be outside, breathing in the fresh air, making space for talking about and doing the real things of life together.

Justin Chung

Justin is a lifestyle and portrait photographer drawn to natural light, the low-key moments of everyday life, and evocative spaces, which he has an abundance of, living in Los Angeles with his wife and two children.

—

Where does your love of the outdoors come from?
I've loved being outdoors since I was young, exploring the Outer Sunset neighborhood and Ocean Beach in San Francisco. Now that my wife and I have two kids, my love of being outdoors has grown even more as I get to spend more time outside with my family.

What's your relationship with the sun?
My relationship with the sun is everything. As a photographer, I am inspired by natural light, and I bring that sensitivity to light into every photograph I take.

How has your relationship with the outdoors affected and informed the way you live in your home?
I love bringing elements of nature into our home. I look for plants, textures, color palettes, and fragrances that evoke the natural world around me.

What do you find to be the true value of gathering around food with friends?
I really feed off the energy of others, and I find that small gatherings around food with friends help recalibrate me.

What kind of food or meal do you most enjoy sitting down to?
Anything home-cooked, especially Korean food.

What's one significant memory or feeling from your childhood surrounding eating with others?
One of my favorite memories from my childhood goes back to our family meals. As a middle child of three boys, as well as with a large extended family close by, I was lucky to experience a full family gathering regularly.

How has seeing and experiencing nature through the lens of photography changed your perspective on it?
Photography has allowed me to appreciate the subtle beauty of nature. Because of photography, I'm always noticing natural lines, negative space, and patches of light when I'm outdoors.

Where do you go to find calm, quiet, and respite from the city's noises?
I love going to places such as Huntington Gardens, beaches, and local canyons, where I can enjoy some quiet, open space for a bit.

What's your go-to way of meeting up with friends outdoors?
A quick hike or a walk on the coast, or if there is time, I love to make coffee to go and enjoy it with friends outdoors.

What gives you energy when spending time in nature?
Disconnecting gives me the most energy out in nature. Being able to just enjoy the scenery and maybe shoot a few rolls of film for myself without worrying about whatever else may be on my mind is something I really cherish.

—

Jamón Serrano with Orange Zest and Olive Oil

This delicious, no-fuss recipe was shared with me by my friend Saehee Cho. In her words, "It is simple, perfect luxury—I love when one simple ingredient transforms a dish. Cured meats are delicious all by themselves, but here orange zest adds so much sweet brightness without the acidity of lemon. This would be beautiful with Manchego, or a soft cheese like burrata— or maybe even thick homemade ricotta."

SERVES 3 OR 4

10 to 15 slices serrano ham

1 orange

2 tablespoons extra-virgin olive oil

Lemon slices for garnish (optional)

Arrange the ham on a serving plate. Grate the zest of the orange over the ham, trying to avoid the bitter white pith. Drizzle with the olive oil. Garnish with slices of the orange or with lemon slices, if desired, and serve.

Ways to Invite the Outdoors In

Even when I can't be out-side, having nature close at hand is essential for my well-being. Here are some foolproof tactics for getting a dose of the outdoors—even when you're stuck at your laptop.

~ Place a large potted tree next to a window in one of your favorite rooms in the house (or better yet, plant a tree outside the window), and enjoy the shadow play on the walls from the leaves throughout the day.

~ If you don't have much of a green thumb and can't keep indoor plants alive, no matter. Find a fallen branch, and put it anywhere in the house in a big vase. Voilà! It will undoubtedly lift your mood.

~ To feel instantly transported to sunnier, more tropical climes, get a fragrant piece of fruit (like a ripe passion fruit, pineapple, or guava) and set it within wafting distance for a pleasant sensory treat.

~ Hang wind chimes outside your door; you'll always know when the breeze is blowing.

~ Make a habit of paying attention as you spend time outside. Look for objects of unusual beauty (such as a rock, a ginkgo leaf, an odd-shaped stick, or an old wasps' nest), and when you feel moved, bring a few home to display somewhere that you'll see in your regular comings and goings.

~ Open the blinds/curtains/shades and let the light in. Keep the windows and doors open when weather permits. Listen to whatever noises float in—crickets, mourning doves, rustling leaves, children playing, the wind.

~ Nothing lifts spirits like being able to see a single bloom or sprig of foliage throughout the day. Clip a bit of whatever's in season in your yard or on your street and put it in some water next to the kitchen sink for a mood-lifter.

~ Spend fifteen minutes in the sun (or better yet, thirty). When you come back inside, you'll carry the sun rays with you.

How to Be Close to Nature Wherever You Live

When I say "close to nature," I picture wringing every last drop out of time spent outdoors. It's about being attuned to the rhythms of the day, greeting the sun with gladness and stealing any chance for a breath of fresh air. It's noticing the setting sun and then pointing out the rising moon. It's bringing home a leaf to admire, or watching a chickadee be its chickadee-self. Being close to nature is being full of wonder, over and over again. It's being aware that our environment plays into our overall sense of well-being and aliveness. Intimacy with nature is the understanding that we live and breathe just like plants; we need sun and air and the right ecosystem (community) to survive and thrive.

Our ability to be close to nature doesn't correspond to having a wealth of resources—or a lack of them. Instead, it's a posture, or an attitude, and the active choice to recognize the riches around us. To make this choice means allowing for a surprising slant of light, perhaps, the buzz of humming bees, a flock of pigeons in flight, the scent of a hot dry field, and so many other tiny, easily overlooked marvels to positively change even a minute of the day. Cultivating this closeness may mean eating dinners on a postage stamp–sized patio. Or taking walks without a phone or earbuds—listening instead to the birds, neighborhood sounds, the chatter of bugs. Or stepping outside your solo house on a hill, far from anyone, to watch the sun move through the clouds yet again.

No matter who you are or where you live, the call to be close to nature does not require grand gestures, changing your zip code, or attending a retreat in the woods. Rather, just open your eyes; open your ears. Open your hands, and you will receive, receive, receive.

Kate McMahon

A dedicated ocean swimmer and a lifelong nature devotee, Kate owns and designs a clothing line of knitwear and modern classics called Covet by Kate.

—

Where does your love of the outdoors come from?
As a family when I was growing up, we spent all of our free time in nature. Camping, backpacking, sailing, horseback riding, river rafting, rock climbing, or hanging out at the beach. My dad was an extreme outdoorsman, while my mom was a "fashionista." He found his joy in the wild; she found hers in shopping. I feel like I am the embodiment of both of their passions. I am most comfortable and alive in nature, and I express my creativity through fashion and design. These two seemingly opposites inform each other and make up the whole of what I do and how I spend my time.

What's your relationship with the sun?
My relationship with the sun is all-important. I seek out the sun every day. I like to eat my meals in the sun. Take naps in the sun. Feel the sun on my skin. It is my ultimate mood elevator.

How do you define well-being? What tangible daily acts do you practice to claim it for yourself?
To me, well-being is feeling fully expressed in all aspects of life; it means living authentically and connecting deeply with family, friends, and community. Achieving well-being is an ongoing practice that, for me, starts with morning journaling, yoga, and being in nature—taking either a hike or a swim in the ocean. The idea is to align with my divine spirit and let it guide my thoughts, words, and actions. If I can get out of my head and into my heart, I feel more content and am able to live life more joyfully.

Laura Dart

Laura is a food, lifestyle, and landscape photographer who chases the light everywhere she goes.

—

Where does your love of the outdoors come from?
I grew up camping a lot, and I was always the first one to sign up for a backpacking trip or excursion in the wilderness when one was offered at school. My first trip out of the country was to Ecuador, where I lived off-grid in the middle of the jungle for a month; I slept outside in a hammock, and I showered under a waterfall. I was drawn more to warmer weather but found myself cooling off by submerging in a lake or the ocean whenever possible. I still dream of living so close to the water that I can swim daily.

What's your relationship with the sun?
The sun is healing to me, and I am always looking for ways to spend more time under it. Obviously, as I get older, I am careful to protect myself from its harmful effects, but I find that a daily dose does wonders for my overall health. Living in Santa Fe means it is sunny here most of the time, and after a long period of living in the rainy Pacific Northwest, I do not take the sun's presence for granted.

How do you define well-being? What tangible daily acts do you practice to claim it for yourself?
Well-being to me is living a balanced lifestyle whenever possible. I was constantly in motion for a long time due to the fast pace of my photography career, and I got pretty out of balance. Living in the desert for the past few years has helped me slow down and find a new rhythm. Having the time and space to meditate, do yoga, be in nature daily, cook with local produce, and create work that I feel good about are some of the positive changes that have come from this season of well-being.

How has your relationship with the outdoors affected and informed the way you live in your home?
My intimate relationship with the outdoors led me to my home of the past two and a half years, a small adobe cottage on ten acres (four hectares) outside of Santa

Fe. There are 360-degree views of the Sangre de Cristos and Jemez Mountains that leave me speechless daily from their beauty. The property is rustic and feels a lot like a campground, giving you a true experience of living in nature. I wake up with the sunrise, birdsong, and light illuminating the surrounding landscape in the most peaceful way. It is truly heaven on earth, and I would stay in this place forever if I could.

What do you find to be the true value of gathering around food with friends?

The tangible energy that you feel in the shared experience. Breaking bread is the purest form of collaboration, and it brings unity in both the physical and spiritual sense. I have made it a part of my lifestyle to host gatherings whenever possible, and I love to meet new people this way.

What in nature brings you joy?

The colors, light, scents, sounds, and having all the senses engaged but also feeling a stillness bring me joy in nature. I am always inspired and feel grounded and pure when I am in nature. My photography work encompasses these elements, as I prefer to shoot in landscape over a studio.

What are your favorite rituals around food and eating with others?

Some of my favorite rituals involve wine and fire. A good bottle of wine, a fire to warm the space or to sit around, and a baguette, some cheese, and olives to share with old or new friends. I find this to be the experience I return to again and again; timeless moments to be repeated and that always make me feel at home. Sharing these simple pleasures outdoors at golden hour is another ritual I take part in quite often, especially in the summer. I have an open lot next to my home where I have "golden-hour wine club" with a friend weekly, and it is one of my favorite rituals.

Where is the most pleasure for you in food? Growing it? Preparing it? Sharing it with others?

The most pleasure for me in food is definitely sharing it. During the past ten years of my life, I have found myself enjoying many unique and beautiful experiences that have food at the center. Being a photographer has given me the unique perspective of both capturing and sharing these intimate moments, from being on tour with the band Mumford & Sons at the beginning of my career to casually ending up eating dinner at René Redzepi's home to getting to photograph an award-winning cookbook, Joshua McFadden's *Six Seasons*, a few years ago. These experiences opened me up to the culinary scene in an intimate way, and I will always return to them as the best memories of my life.

What's one significant memory or feeling from your childhood surrounding eating with others?

Unfortunately, I did not grow up with many good food memories, which is probably why I have been so adamant about creating my own! The one thing that I remember being really special in regard to food would be mushroom hunting with my grandpa. We only went a handful of times, but we were on the hunt for morels. He was a really good hunter, and he also had an amazing garden that I remember going to as a child. We froze the mushrooms we found and saved them for Christmas-morning breakfast. Every time I eat morels, I think of him and am transported back to that place in time.

What does watching the sunrise or sunset offer to your mental, spiritual, even physical well-being?

There's a place on the property where I live that I have designated the Sunset Spot. There is the most beautiful sunset there every night, and watching it is my daily meditation. The sunsets are paintings that could be viewed for hours as they shift in color, light, and perspective. I have more sunset photos from this time than anything else. The sky is my favorite thing about New Mexico.

Jessica and Justin Donais

Jessica and Justin left their longtime home of Los Angeles to open their own Sicilian-inspired pizza joint in Portland, Oregon, where Jessica continues to run her own branding, design, and consulting studio, Marbury, and Justin works as a cinematographer.

—

Where does your love of the outdoors come from?
Jessica (JCD): I spent a lot of time outdoors as a kid, rolling around in the grass with my sisters, playing with the flowers my mom planted in our front yard, scooping tadpoles out of the stream in the park down the street from our house. A trip to Will Rogers Beach was a frequent weekend activity for my family; we would spend hours in the sand and go home tired and sun-kissed. I think these times forged my association between the outdoors and happiness and relaxation.

What's your relationship with the sun?
JCD: It is the rhythm by which I live my days. I wake up to the sun streaming through our bedroom windows, I find beauty in the way it bounces off the walls of our house throughout the day, and I begin to turn inward as it falls behind the mountains in the evening. Especially now, living in a grayer climate than the one I grew up in, the sight of the sun gives me a real zest for life.

How do you define well-being? What tangible daily acts do you practice to claim it for yourself?
JCD: Well-being means honoring that little voice in your head that tells you exactly what it needs. It means resting when rest feels needed, carving out alone time when solitude feels needed, getting outdoors when clarity feels needed, and forgoing work when connection with loved ones feels needed. It's understanding that these practices are integral to feeling whole.

How has your relationship with the outdoors affected and informed the way you live in your home?
Justin (JLD): For me, choosing a place to live always begins with the sun's path. Figuring out where the sun will rise and set, and at what time of day, and how that

will change with the seasons, and, as a result, affect the feeling of the house. I really love having morning light where the sunrise can wake you up naturally.

JCD: I think because I equate being outdoors with feeling calm and grounded, when I bring any element of nature indoors, it achieves a similar feeling for me. Something as simple as a vase filled with flowers picked on a walk around the neighborhood has the ability to transform my mood. So an abundance of houseplants, fresh flowers, and natural materials are my go-tos when it comes to creating the home I want to live in.

What do you find to be the true value of gathering around food with friends?

JLD: The human connection. It's the ultimate sense of community. Being surrounded by good friends just amplifies the pleasures of a delicious meal.

JCD: I agree that it's about connection. I think food is often simply a vehicle to bring people together to feel a sense of joy and belonging. It's hard to find community these days, but gathering for a meal seems like the one thing we can always do to show our love and appreciation for each other.

What in nature brings you joy?

JCD: Now that I live somewhere with seasons, nature has brought me a level of joy unlike anything I ever experienced in Los Angeles. I always say it feels like nature is putting on a show for us. Some of my favorite flowers bloom for only a few weeks each year before their petals fall, so it's a real practice in being present to stop and take in the beauty while it lasts. It reminds me that everything is fleeting, but also that you never know what lies around the corner.

What are your favorite rituals around food and eating with others?

JCD: Once Friday rolls around, I'm always eager to open our doors to friends or family to share an impromptu meal. We have some friends that we meet with on Sunday mornings to enjoy different coffee and pastry spots around town, and others that we can always

count on to go on a food adventure with us. There is no relaxing or social time for us that doesn't involve food.

What kind of food or meal do you most enjoy sitting down to?

JLD: Any meal with bread. From baguette to pizza to pita to roti—so many cultures have done amazing things with wheat. They're all delicious, but the history of how those foods came to be is equally exciting to me.

JCD: I always want to nosh on a little bit of everything, so my favorite meals tend to be potluck-style, where you can fill your plate with small bites of many different things. Some of my favorite meals have been ones when we picked a theme and everyone brought their own interpretation of it. I love getting inspired by how other people cook and taking home new recipes.

What's one significant memory or feeling from your childhood surrounding eating with others?

JLD: Growing up in an Italian family—it was always loud and always delicious.

JCD: I grew up with my family hosting Thanksgiving for our extended family every year, so we always had a full house and a *lot* of food. I think that's when I first learned the power of the elastic waistband.

How has your relationship to nature shifted as you've made the move from a perennially sunny place (Los Angeles) to a place more well known for its frequent rain and clouds (Portland)?

JCD: I think I've become a lot more in tune with the cycles of nature. It was always hard to slow down in Los Angeles, because there was never really a reason to stay indoors and just do nothing. But living in Portland, I really appreciate how there are seasons for seizing the sunny moments and seasons for slowing down. It helps me pace myself and conserve my energy in a way that I never have done before.

—

Sfincione
(Sicilian style pizza)

The beauty of this recipe is that you can't mess it up. Every household in Sicily has its own family version of sfincione, a Sicilian street food that loosely translates to "thick sponge" in reference to its bread base. The thick slab of bread is often topped with tomato sauce or just cheese based on the region. Anchovies and bread crumbs tend to make their way onto the toppings too. This recipe is the classic version that you can find on the streets of Palermo, and what we served at our first pizza spot, Pizza Doughnais.

MAKES 8 SQUARES;
SERVES 4 TO 8

A ball (1¾ to 2¼ pounds/800 g to 1 kg) of your favorite focaccia or pizza dough

Extra-virgin olive oil

One 15-ounce (425 g) can crushed tomatoes

1⅓ teaspoons sea salt

⅔ teaspoon granulated garlic

1 tablespoon dried basil

1½ teaspoons dried rosemary

1½ teaspoons dried oregano, plus more for sprinkling

1½ teaspoons dried marjoram

½ teaspoon pepper

1¼ cups (125 g) bread crumbs

14 anchovy fillets

1 large yellow onion (optional)

¼ cup grated (25 g) Pecorino Romano cheese

The first thing you'll want to do is find your favorite focaccia recipe to use as the basis for the dough. You'll want to end up with 1¾ to 2¼ pounds (800 g to 1 kg) worth of finished dough, whether you make it yourself or buy it somewhere (you can ask your favorite pizzeria if they'll sell you some). Once the dough is proofed over halfway, then you'll be ready to move it into the pan.

Pour 3 tablespoons olive oil onto a half sheet pan (13 by 18 inches/ 33 by 46 cm) and spread it out to coat the pan evenly. (If it seems like too much oil, it's probably the right amount; as the dough bakes, the oil will fry the bottom of it in the pan.) Place the dough in the center of the oily pan. Rub your clean hands with a generous amount of olive oil and press out the dough to cover the entire pan. Be gentle! The dough will snap back and shrink, but that's normal; let it rest for 15 minutes whenever this happens and then press it out a little more; you will probably need to repeat this process 3 to 5 times until the dough is fully relaxed, covering the entire pan. Be sure to cover the dough with plastic wrap to keep it from drying out, and then place it in the fridge overnight.

Meanwhile, make the sauce: Pour the crushed tomatoes into a medium bowl. Combine the salt, garlic, dried herbs, and pepper and mix into the tomatoes. Cover and place in the fridge overnight.

Put the bread crumbs in a bowl, then use your clean hands to mash up 6 of the anchovies, one at a time. Once they have become paste-like, add to the bread crumbs and mix everything together. Take any olive oil remaining in the tin that was previously holding your anchovies and pour it into the bread-crumb mixture. Refill the can with olive oil as necessary so that none of the remaining anchovies are exposed to the air. Cover and place the bowl in the fridge overnight.

The next day, heat the oven to 450°F (230°C). Take the pan with the dough out of the fridge. Place it in a warm area, or even on top of your preheating oven. The time the dough will rest depends on the temperature in your kitchen, but once you see that the dough has puffed up like a cloud and almost tripled in height, you're ready to bake! Slide the risen dough into the oven and bake for about 70 percent of the time given in your recipe or on the bag of dough, or until you start to see some coloration on top, probably 10 to 15 minutes. (The amount of water in the dough will dictate the bake time, but you want to cook it through nicely.) Remove from the oven.

At this point, you can let the crust cool and wait until guests arrive to finish it, or just go right ahead to the next step. In either case, heat your oven to the highest temperature possible: 500 to 550°F (260 to 290°C).

At this stage, if you want to add the onion, dice it and let cook it in a little olive oil in a saucepan until translucent. Remove from the heat. (At the pizzeria, sometimes we'd add caramelized onions to our bread crumbs, but leaving the onion out entirely is okay too.)

Because the dough has already set in the oven, you can be generous with the toppings. Ladle the sauce evenly over the dough. Scatter the onions over the sauce if you have them. Scoop up a handful of your anchovy bread crumbs and scatter them evenly over the sauce.

Slide the sfincione back into the oven and bake until the crust turns a beautiful golden brown, 10 to 12 minutes.

Pull the sfincione out of the oven, carefully remove it from the hot pan, and place it on a cooling rack. (The rack will keep the bottom from getting soggy.)

The secret here is to add the rest of the toppings while the crust is hot out of the oven so that the steam will activate all the flavors. Sprinkle some dried oregano over the hot bread crumbs, and then finish with the Pecorino Romano. Lastly, slice the sfincione into 8 slices and add an anchovy fillet to each slice.

Let the sfincione rest on the rack for 2 to 4 minutes, then *mangia!*

Cristiana Sadigianis

Cristiana, a photo producer turned olive oil purveyor, drew on her Greek heritage and summers on Andros—as a child and today—to create Oracle Oil, a beautiful venture she says is an ode to her grandparents and their inspiring, enduring way of life.

—

Where does your love of the outdoors come from?
Both my parents were born and raised in Greece—my mother in the mountains of Delphi and my father on the Aegean Sea on the Peloponnese peninsula. Growing up, I spent every summer on my grandparents' farms, harvesting olives, shelling almonds, and picking wild figs. From a young age, I became quite comfortable with the cicadas' persistent hum, and early-rising sheep. I understood the value of living off the land and alongside the natural growth cycles of the food we ate. I also loved hiking in the mountains and swimming solo in the ocean out to faraway rocks.

What's your relationship with the sun?
The sun runs deep in my DNA! I feel alive, focused, and energized by it. I think it makes sense, given my deep Greek agrarian roots, as my ancestors spent a lot of time outdoors. On a more practical level, we in the United States are a nation deficient in vitamin D due to our long days sitting inside at computers, so I welcome any opportunity to be in the sun's embrace.

How do you define well-being? What tangible daily acts do you practice to claim it for yourself?
Well-being for me is a state of presence, connection, and ease. If I can think clearly and feel strong and connected to my body, then I can create, find purpose, and connect with others. Some of my daily practices include meditation (sometimes Transcendental Meditation, other days simply walking on the beach), an infrared sauna, supplements and herbs, movement—depending on my environment, dancing, hiking, swimming, or yoga. I also value preparing every aspect of our meals through gardening, cooking, and setting the table, and listening to music, mostly reggae. I also try to surround myself

The act of growing, harvesting, and pressing olives feels so inherently down-to-earth. What drew you to develop an olive oil company?

It really goes back to my grandparents again! Oracle is an ode to them. I think being exposed to the harvests each season, whether it was olives, or grapes for wine, or apricots for jam, left a mark on me. We would barter with other families in the small local communities for the goods they grew. Looking back, it was a really beautiful tradition of growing seasonally and sharing the bounty. My grandparents and their ancestors were stewards of the land, and when I was growing up in that way, among our own bees, almonds, chickens, and olives, I didn't realize that this wasn't the norm and was not as easily found outside of those small communities in Greece. I wanted that narrative to come through in creating Oracle.

What brings you back to yourself when life has gotten a bit too busy or frenzied?

Meditation, making a cup of matcha with homemade almond milk, putting on music and moving, the sea, and eating copious amounts of dark chocolate!

How has your heritage influenced the way you think about food and sharing it with others?

My Greek heritage has been the driving force behind all things food and community for me, from how carefully the food was grown and then prepared with love and attention to whom I'm sharing it with and how. In Greece, you start planning tomorrow's lunch while you are still eating today's. And everyone is always invited! If you're walking by someone's house and they're cooking outside, they beckon you over to eat—they don't even need to know you, and they get offended if you say no!

It's also the case that the size of the fridge in most Greek households is tiny compared with the ones we have in the United States, the reason being that everything you eat has either been picked from your garden that morning or bought fresh from the fisherman or butcher. The idea of freezing food is not very common in Greek culture! What I find most special is that all meals are eaten outside—with a view of a craggy mountain, a grazing goat, and the Mediterranean as your backdrop—while sitting under a grapevine trellis, next to a citrus grove, or under the shade of a great big old, wise olive tree.

—

Gemista (Greek Stuffed Vegetables)

SERVES 6 TO 12

6 large firm but ripe tomatoes (a combination of red, yellow, and orange if available)

6 medium firm eggplants or round zucchini

¼ cup (60 ml) extra-virgin olive oil

3 large onions, finely chopped

5 to 6 scallions, finely chopped

1 cup (195 g) medium-grain white rice

2 garlic cloves, finely chopped

⅓ cup (45 g) lightly toasted pine nuts

¾ cup (180 ml) water

Sea salt and pepper

¼ cup (15 g) chopped flat-leaf parsley

½ cup (30 g) chopped mint

Pinch of dried oregano

½ cup (25 g) chopped dill

½ teaspoon ground nutmeg

Wash the vegetables. Take a very sharp knife and slice off the top of each tomato and eggplant or zucchini; keep each vegetable and its cap together. With a sharp teaspoon, gently scoop out the pulp of each vegetable, being careful not to tear the outer skin and leaving a shell about ½ inch (1 cm) thick. Remove the seeds from all vegetables used, chop the pulp, and place the pulp, with the juices, in a large bowl.

Preheat the oven to 350°F (175°C). Heat 2 tablespoons of the olive oil in a large heavy skillet over medium heat. Add the onions and scallions and sauté, stirring occasionally, until translucent and soft, about 10 minutes. Add the rice and cook, stirring frequently, for 3 to 4 minutes. Add the tomato and eggplant or zucchini pulp, the garlic, pine nuts, and water, then reduce the heat, cover the skillet, and simmer for 5 to 7 minutes, until the rice has started to soften and most of the liquid has been absorbed (the mixture should still be moist). Season the mixture with salt and pepper and stir in the herbs and nutmeg. Remove from the heat.

Stuff the vegetables with the rice filling and crown with their caps. Place in a baking pan. Add about ¼ cup (60 ml) water to the pan and drizzle the remaining 2 tablespoons olive oil over the vegetables. Bake for 50 minutes to 1 hour, until the vegetables are soft and blistery and the rice is tender. Baste with the pan juices during baking if necessary. Serve hot or cold.

There's something so ancient and simple about sharing food at the same table that we often take for granted how symbolic and powerful it can be to eat with other people.

—Saehee Cho

GATHERING FOR EXTRA-SPECIAL OCCASIONS

What makes for an extra-special occasion? Any moment, milestone, or life event can become a joyous affair. It doesn't take much to turn an everyday happening into something that feels more set apart and celebratory—no fireworks, gobs of money, or hired entertainment necessary. Whether you choose a special place, a standout group of people, or a bit of additional decor, even the simplest gathering can be transformed into something almost ceremonial by anointing the moment with a hint of extra care.

Lighted candles can instantly elevate the mood. As can a sheaf of wildflowers or grasses plunked into a jar. A favorite tablecloth. Maybe music. A magical setting under a tree, by a river, or within the intimacy of your own backyard. While the world tells us we must go all out every time we want to celebrate something special, nature tells us there's a celebration happening around us all the time and we only need to join in the dance—swaying trees, birds bursting with song, the light shifting around us at every moment. Just the *being together* brings us joy, and being out-of-doors with the sun and a breeze and the clouds above can make the occasion that much more exceptional.

I like to begin my day in the garden with a cup of tea and end the day in the garden with a glass of wine. That's a pretty perfect scenario: solitude, nature, all the senses in play.

Phoebe Cole-Smith

Saehee Cho

Saehee is a writer, chef, and food stylist, and the founder of the collaborative produce and grocery delivery service Soon Mini.

—

Where does your love of the outdoors come from?
I'm a California girl through and through. I grew up adjacent to Laguna Beach, went to school in Santa Cruz and San Diego, and eventually ended up in Los Angeles. The beach has always been no more than a thirty-minute drive away, and I find it hard to imagine a life where I didn't have easy access to a large body of water.

How do you define well-being? What tangible daily acts do you practice to claim it for yourself?
In my perfect world, I am reserving my early-morning hours for writing. The few rare periods of balance in my life have been marked by the luxury of enough mind space for my writing practice. Starting my day with the simple act of writing five hundred words helps me find meaning and intention in the rest of my day. It creates a tone, and a structure that I then get to occupy.

How has your relationship with the outdoors affected and informed the way you live in your home?
In a way, I feel like I live outdoors and just sleep indoors! I take most of my meals outside in my garden. I don't even have a proper dining table in my house, because other than on a rainy day (and even then!), it feels preferable to eat with an open sky above me.

What do you find to be the true value of gathering around food with friends?
There's something so ancient and simple about sharing food at the same table that we often take for granted how symbolic and powerful it can be to eat with other people. It's an inherently communal act—passing plates, pouring wine, serving one another. It also slows us all down to the same pace and puts everyone at the table on the same level.

I see this almost anytime I'm at a gathering of new people. What starts out nervous and slightly awkward gets salved throughout the meal by the very human act of eating together. The appetizers get people acquainted

Tina's Special Dipping Sauce

MAKES 1 CUP (240 ML)

4 to 5 fresh red chilies, finely chopped (use Thai, Vietnamese, or other medium-hot chilies)

¼ cup (60 ml) boiling water

3 tablespoons sugar

¼ cup (60 ml) fish sauce

2 teaspoons minced ginger

¼ cup (60 ml) lime juice

Put the chilies in a small heatproof bowl, cover with the boiling water, and let sit for 2 minutes or so to release some of their red color.

Add the sugar and stir to dissolve. Add the fish sauce, ginger, and lime juice and stir until incorporated. Let cool to room temperature, then cover and store in an airtight container in the refrigerator for up to a week.

Serve as a condiment for rice or as a dipping sauce.

Molly Sedlacek

Molly is the founder and creative director of OR.CA Landscape Design. Her distinct approach to working with plants and spaces feels intuitive, reverent, and wholly welcoming.

—

Where does your love of the outdoors come from?
My mother is a landscape designer and contractor. My father worked for the US Forest Service, was a wildfire firefighter, and farmed bamboo. My sister and I were surrounded by the life cycle of seeds and the impacts of the seasons: summer (fragrance), fall (fire), winter (reflection), and spring (birth). The outdoors is the blueprint of my story.

What's your relationship with the sun?
I left home in search of the sun. There's nothing like the Oregon Coast: vast, rich, big, bold. But to be all of these things, the land needs a lot of rain. So I headed south to California.

After a decade of living in California, I rarely eat inside anymore. My body has become accustomed to absorbing as much sunlight as possible. Sun fills my soul.

How do you define well-being? What tangible daily acts do you practice to claim it for yourself?
Rituals contribute to my well-being: there is an exchange of energy out and energy in. I start every day by hiking with my dog, Bear. We climb to the top of a hill in Fairfax to see the sunrise. Afterward, I burn a half stick of copal, put on the radio, drink two cups of coffee, and dive deep into the world of OR.CA. Stimulation of the mind—whether from physical movement, sensory input, or curiosity—is very important to my well-being.

How has your relationship with the outdoors affected and informed the way you live in your home?
There are very few things in my home that can't go outdoors. My friends joke about my furnishing choices, as there is an actual boulder in one room. Nothing in my home is precious, mass produced, or light. Beauty to me is untouched materials, in their raw and natural form

(meaning they are often heavy). They have not been purchased but rather collected and gathered over time. This is what creates the notion of home for me.

What do you find to be the true value of gathering around food with friends?

There's a warmth to gathering around food that is really only captured when a table is set. There's a glow in the air, and everyone is smiling. Coming together over common interests and sharing our stories is one of the most important things in life.

What in nature brings you joy?

The composition Mother Nature displays in everything she creates. A decaying log is one of the most beautiful sights. The rotting brown bark is giving life to mossy green, and new growth spews out like a bouquet. There's so much poetry in even the smallest fragment of nature. Humans have a tendency to complicate things. Nature simply exists and emits joy everywhere we look.

What are your favorite rituals around food and eating with others?

A table with the patina of age, set with objects of conversation: textiles, candles, incense, floral decor, natural elements—all arranged thoughtfully to accompany the food.

What's one significant memory or feeling from your childhood surrounding eating with others?

Spending time together at a meal was not common for me as a child. My parents both worked a lot, and when we were all home, every ounce of daylight was used for working in the garden. However, on Sundays, my mom would make breakfast. It was such a treat to wake up to the smell of crepes served with berries from the garden, all of us together.

How did you find your way to landscape design, and how has your work in and with the outdoors changed or altered your experience with nature?

Even before starting my business, I found myself spending every spare moment tending to my own garden. I had subconsciously learned during my childhood that there was always a weed to pluck or a plant to tend to. And through this ritual, the garden kept getting better, and my design style began to take shape.

Landscape design has profoundly deepened my connection to nature. I look at colors, materials, and shapes very intimately because I've learned that through practice, we can form thoughts and share ideas through working with natural materials.

You talk about your work as being for "life without walls." How does the concept of enjoying life without walls manifest itself in your own daily rhythms?

This goes back to the question about the sun. I find that I absorb experiences more when I'm outdoors: a song, a glass of wine, a conversation outdoors, without walls, heightens my senses.

Your work feels so in tune with the natural world. Have you always thought about working with outdoor spaces and landscapes in the way that you do now?

Whether I recognized it or not, I think this work has been a part of me for my entire life. It started when I was building forts using only what was available in the forest behind our house, or watching my mom weave wreaths, and seeing my dad dry bamboo poles to make fencing. This is what interests me most about landscape design: approaching each project through a lens of innocence. Anything is possible if we put constraints aside and fully embrace imagination.

What makes a designed outdoor space meaningful for you?

The people who occupy it. Being able to see the humans the garden was built for actually *live* in the space is why I do this work. Kids running in the woods, adults placing wineglasses on the table, a firepit being ignited as the evening starts to wind down: These gardens are an extension of our homes: they are as important as the walls that protect us and the roofs over our heads.

—

THE OUTDOORS IS THE BLUEPRINT OF MY STORY.

Stillwater Restaurant Sweet-and-Sour Vinaigrette

A quick, easy vinaigrette for dressing up any simple salad.

MAKES ABOUT 4 CUPS (1 L)

2 cups (480 ml) Mae Ploy sweet chili sauce

1½ cups (355 ml) rice wine vinegar

2 tablespoons tamari or soy sauce

¼ cup (60 ml) Asian sesame oil

3 tablespoons chopped ginger

Combine the chili sauce, vinegar, tamari, sesame oil, and ginger in a large jar or a bowl and mix well. Store in the fridge until ready to use. Shake or stir before using.

Ordinary Things *to* Make Any Place Extraordinary

Many of us have the idea we need to use proper "decor" to spruce up the house or the table. Nonsense! Objects of beauty abound in nature and provide a visual thrill when we use them in unsuspecting ways.

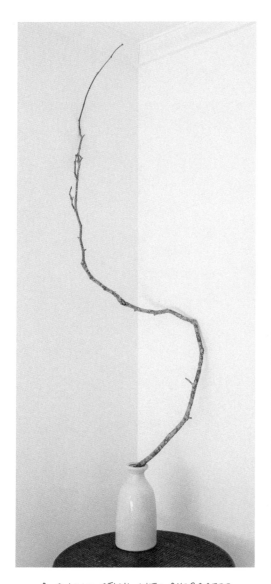

A SINGLE STICK WITH CHARACTER

A SURPRISING COMBINATION OF YARD CLIPPINGS

TREASURES FROM THE SEA

A VERY ELEGANT PLACE SETTING
(A NASTURTIUM LEAF)

A WEED-SCULPTURE WITH SOME HELP FROM A WELL-PLACED ROCK HOLE

Phoebe Cole-Smith

Phoebe is a farmer-chef who runs Dirt Road Farm with her husband, Mike, in Weston, Connecticut, where they host farm-to-table suppers and private culinary experiences. Together, they tap their sugar maple trees to produce yearly batches of syrup.

—

Where does your love of the outdoors come from?
From my mother. Not only did she spend time outside with me throughout my childhood, but she also taught me how to look for and really see the beauty in nature. She was a painter, who effortlessly shared how she saw the world, and what she noticed. And she always saw the beauty in things—the same way she always saw the good in people.

For what occasion do you most enjoy gathering around food with friends?
To celebrate whatever season we are in. Reaping the rewards of what's growing in the garden, in the fields, or in the wild by preparing it and sharing it is the ultimate act of nurturing and generosity, the greatest life-affirming act we can share with one another. It is almost a form of prayer—an acknowledgment of the benevolence of nature, which provides us with sustenance and happiness.

How do you define well-being? What tangible daily acts do you practice to claim it for yourself?
Well-being for me has to do with balance in my life, somewhat similar to balance in a recipe: the right ratio between work and play, between solitude and socializing, between movement and stillness, like the right balance between tart and sweet, between acidity and alkalinity. Getting outside every day is a necessity for me—I move more than I sit, because of the nature of my work, of course, but also by choice. Mike and I walk every day with our dogs, taking the same route, seeing different trees and wildlife and sky every time. Repetition need not be boring. I am in the gardens all the time during the growing season, and in the cold winter woods during the sugaring season.

What's your favorite scent in nature that immediately transports you to a different time and place?

Being in a meadow with the heady scent of wildflowers, grass, and greenery warmed by a midsummer sun brings me back to the meadows of my Illinois childhood. I recall picking daisies with my mom; making clover crowns and necklaces to wear; lying on my back and breathing in that blossomy, grassy, earthy fragrance while looking up at the billowing, shape-shifting, fair-weather clouds.

How has your relationship with the outdoors affected and informed the way you live in your home?

Our home is an indoor/outdoor place; everything is open to the outside when the weather allows it, though obviously that's not year-round here in Connecticut. We live on the patio outside our kitchen during the spring and summer months and well into the fall: We read the paper, drink our morning tea, eat our meals, have our cocktails and wine, and sip our tisanes at the end of the evening. We even work on our laptops at the table under our grape arbor. The grapevines fill in perfectly at just about the time of year it gets hot and we are ready for shade.

What in nature brings you joy?

The change of seasons brings me joy. When the cold brown earth and gray, leafless trees of winter give over to the swelling of growth and faint chartreuse leaves and tiny green sprouts and pale blossoms of early spring, I feel like I might explode from the excitement it all stirs in me. I don't think I could ever live anywhere where there is no real change of seasons.

What kind of food or meal do you most enjoy sitting down to?

A bountiful meal that speaks to the season, that is authentic to the culture and geography in which it was produced, that lets each ingredient shine, and that is presented in a relaxed, unfussy but beautiful way, with attention paid to the details.

What's one significant memory or feeling from your childhood surrounding eating with others?

Again, I think of my mom, and although I'm from a big family, my clearest memories are of eating with her, just the two of us: When I would ride my bike home from school for a lunch of Scotch broth (canned) and cream-cheese-and-jelly sandwiches and she would read to me while I ate, or when we'd eat fried-egg sandwiches in our rowboat on Eel Pond on Martha's Vineyard, or share beef fondue in the '60s when it was just us at home (I was the youngest) after her divorce from my dad.

Straddling the line between farmer and chef means you get the wisdom of each field to inform the other. What has the knowledge you've gained from both of these vocations brought to the rest of your life?

I've learned that the long, hard way pays off—taking the time to coax the very best result out of a plant or an ingredient will always be worth it. And knowing that there is beauty and value in the process and in the work itself.

How do you most regularly choose to recharge outdoors?

I like to begin my day in the garden with a cup of tea and end the day in the garden with a glass of wine. That's a pretty perfect scenario: solitude, nature, all the senses in play.

Do you have any role models whose relationship to nature you find inspiring?

I'm a big fan of the cook and writer Nigel Slater. He is a gardener too, with a tiny-but-burgeoning garden behind his London town house. He is extremely tuned in to the seasons by his connection to what's growing there throughout the year, and as a cook and gardener myself, I deeply identify with his mindful approach to cooking.

In what ways has your relationship to nature changed or evolved as you've grown older?

As I've aged, I've come to respect and to be humbled by nature more than ever. The benevolence, the fury, and the predictable as much as the unforeseeable. It's so much larger than us; I'm lucky to live so close to nature.

—

Rhubarb and Red Currant Fool

The beauty of this very simple, adaptable recipe is that it celebrates any fruit in season—strawberries, blueberries, raspberries, peaches, apples, or pears. I like the juxtaposition of the roasted flavor with something fresh—edible flowers like chamomile and dianthus are a beautiful touch, as are fresh herbs, such as mint, blue African basil, or tarragon. Instead of the maple syrup in the whipped cream, you can use honey or sugar.

SERVES 6 TO 8

1½ pounds (680 g) rhubarb, trimmed of any leaves (which are poisonous) and roughly chopped, tough root ends reserved

1¼ cups (250 g) sugar

2 cups (480 ml) heavy cream

Maple syrup

Several bunches red currants, removed from their stems

Mint leaves and edible flowers for garnish

Preheat the oven to 350°F (175°C). Toss the rhubarb (except for the reserved ends) with 1 cup (200 g) of the sugar in a bowl, then spread out on a rimmed baking sheet. Roast the rhubarb for about 20 minutes, until it is tender but still holds its shape.

Transfer the rhubarb and any juices to a bowl and let cool, then cover and refrigerate until chilled.

Meanwhile, combine the reserved rhubarb ends and the remaining ¼ cup (50 g) sugar in a small saucepan. Add a few splashes of water and bring to a simmer, then cook, stirring occasionally, until very tender, 7 to 10 minutes. Strain the rhubarb through a fine-mesh sieve set over a bowl, pressing on the solids to release as much liquid as possible; discard the pulp and set the syrup aside.

Whip the heavy cream in a large bowl until soft peaks form. Fold in maple syrup to taste and whip just until stiff peaks form. Refrigerate until ready to use.

To assemble the fool, put a spoonful of the roasted rhubarb in the bottom of an 8-ounce (240 ml) glass jar and add a sprinkling of currants, drizzling on a little of the rhubarb syrup if the roasted rhubarb seems dry. Add a big spoonful of whipped cream and continue layering the ingredients, alternating fruit and cream and ending with fruit on top.

Garnish the fool with torn mint leaves and edible flowers, top with a little more fruit and rhubarb syrup, and add a drizzle of maple syrup, if desired. Serve immediately, or cover and refrigerate for up to 4 hours.

Edie Caldwell

Edie has owned antiques stores and art galleries in California and Maine. She enjoys dreaming up future creative ventures and swimming daily.

—

Where does your love of the outdoors come from?
I grew up in Nashville in the 1950s and '60s, which was a wondrous time. When I was a child, I would take off after breakfast—by myself—to explore, climb trees, wade in the creek, and visit my cousins and grandparents, who lived nearby. I'd go home for lunch, then take off again. In the late afternoon, the one streetlight in the neighborhood would come on, and that meant it was time to go home.

What's your relationship with the sun?
Appreciative and cautious.

How do you define well-being? What tangible daily acts do you practice to claim it for yourself?
I am blessed that I get to swim in a pool for thirty to forty minutes every day.

You told me that you moved to Santa Barbara so you could swim in a pool year-round. When did you start swimming and what has motivated you to keep it up?
I started swimming underwater, doing the breaststroke, when I was two years old. I was probably three or four when I started swimming on the surface. I still swim underwater at first, then on the surface for the duration. All I have to do is dive under the water with my eyes open, and I come up absolutely refreshed.

What in nature brings you joy?
Full moons, rainbows, sunsets, and lightning storms.

Where is the most pleasure for you in food? Growing it? Preparing it? Sharing it with others?
I love the adventure and discovery of eating alone in great restaurants, anywhere in the world.

What's one significant memory or feeling from your childhood surrounding eating with others?
I have four brothers and sisters, and when we were children, we ate dinner much earlier than our parents did.

Bismarck (also known as a Dutch Baby)

This puffy pancake is something we always made for special occasions in our family, so enjoying it together always feels like an exceptional event!

SERVES 3

8 tablespoons (1 stick/113 g) unsalted butter, cut into chunks

½ cup (120 ml) milk

½ cup (65 g) unbleached all-purpose flour

2 large (100 g) eggs

Fresh lemon juice for sprinkling

Fresh seasonal fruit (optional)

Confectioners' sugar for dusting

Preheat the oven to 475°F (250°C). Put the butter in a heavy oven-proof frying pan or a shallow baking dish and set it in the oven to melt.

Meanwhile, combine the milk, flour, and eggs in a bowl and whisk gently to make a batter.

When the butter has melted, add the batter to the pan. Return it to the oven and bake for 12 minutes, or until puffed up and just lightly browned. Transfer the Bismarck to a serving plate.

Pour a little of the melted butter remaining in the pan over the pancake and sprinkle on a little lemon juice to taste. Add a bit of fruit, if using, then roll up like a loose jelly roll, sprinkle with confectioners' sugar, and top with more fruit, if desired. Serve immediately.

Sofya Mitchell

Sofya is a chef, writer, and wellness coach based between Scotland and London.

—

Where does your love of the outdoors come from?

From my dad. My parents got divorced when I was young, and he then moved into a seventeenth-century cottage in the Scottish countryside. He had ducks and chickens in a huge, wild garden, and the whole thing backed onto a field. When I used to visit him, we'd light enormous bonfires, bother the ducks, eat eggs gathered straight from the chicken coop, and run around with his border collie puppy. It was such a change from my city life, and something that has definitely stuck with me.

What's your relationship with the sun?

The sun represents one thing to me: life. Like every other thing on this planet, humans are solar powered! What separates us from a sunflower bending toward the rays, or a cat lazily following spots of light around the house, is that we're the only ones to have forgotten our ties to the sun. It's everything. I spend as much time in it as I can!

How do you define well-being? What tangible daily acts do you practice to claim it for yourself?

Well-being, to me, is never one place or act or moment in time. After experiencing severe chronic illness in my early twenties, and healing from it, I had to come to terms with the reality of things: Health is never something that you just suddenly achieve. It's an ongoing process, full of ups and downs, something that never quite ends. You have to dedicate every single day to your habits and rituals. Build on them, immerse yourself in them, let the benefits compound. Stretching, cooking for my family, walking, playing with my dogs, keeping my space beautiful, and eating mindfully are all things that I do daily to feel my best.

What in nature brings you joy?

I love how simple and honest it is. It brings you back from all the nonsense that doesn't actually matter very much, and reminds you of who and what you are. Like it or not, we're as much a part of nature as a sapling or an insect is. It humbles and centers us all at once.

What is your favorite meal for a spontaneous picnic or backyard meal at home?

Seafood is always a good bet for a last-minute outdoor meal! It seems fussy, and it's tempting to reach for more familiar barbecue proteins such as chicken, but fish or shellfish can be cooked in a matter of minutes and always tastes incredible even with minimal seasoning. A whole fish complete with head and fins, or fat prawns with their shells still on, also just looks so beautiful and celebratory. All they need is one or two simple sides, and you're done!

What's one significant memory or feeling from your childhood surrounding eating with others?

Some of my best food memories come from my grandparents. My Scottish father's parents died before I was born, but I have hazy, humid, sun-drenched memories of meals in Singapore with my mother's parents. Every holiday in Southeast Asia would be full of sticky-sweet tropical fruit (mangosteen are my favorite), the funk of fermented shrimp and dried anchovies, freshly pressed sugarcane juice, satay and rojak and roti prata at bustling hawker stalls, homemade curries and soups and noodle dishes at Grandma's house. Everything in Singapore was in Technicolor compared with the muted palette of Scotland.

What makes you feel connected to the outdoors even when you can't physically be outside?

I allow myself the luxury of flowers. Big grand bouquets or little stems of wildflowers, I love them all, and I'm very grateful for how they immediately make any room feel airy and alive. When you pair them with natural materials (real floorboards, sheepskin rugs, antique wooden furniture), you always feel connected to the earth.

Where do you go outdoors when you need to clear your mind and spirit?

I feel most at home in any forest or woodland. Trees are vastly underrated creatures and far cleverer than we give them credit for. They are living temples. Some people find forests too still, too quiet, too dark, even slightly foreboding, but I love being engulfed by the trunks and the canopies and the dappled sunlight spilling through onto the ground. There isn't anything better than the smell of damp wood and moss. I'm awful and impatient at meditating in a boxy room, but I could sit in the woods silently all by myself for hours.

—

Kerala-Style Grilled Fish in Fig Leaves (Meen Pollichathu)

I love fish on the grill. It's quick and easy and always feels special. The masala can be made a day in advance, so all you have to do before everyone arrives is throw together a couple of sides. If you can't get whole fish, you can use fillets. You just want a firm-fleshed fish that'll stand up well to grilling. Traditionally this recipe is made using banana leaves, but fig leaves smell sweet and slightly coconutty, so they work beautifully with South Indian flavors.

SERVES 2

MASALA MIXTURE

2 tablespoons virgin coconut oil

12 to 15 curry leaves

1 tablespoon mustard seeds

4 large shallots or 2 small onions, finely sliced

2 thumb-sized pieces of ginger, finely chopped

4 cloves garlic, finely chopped

2 large green chilies (medium heat), sliced

2 medium tomatoes, diced

¼ teaspoon turmeric powder

1 teaspoon Kashmiri chili powder

1 teaspoon coriander powder

1 teaspoon garam masala

1 tablespoon tamarind paste with seeds, steeped in a small amount of water

1 tablespoon coconut sugar or jaggery

Salt

2 whole sea bass, scaled and gutted

6 large fig leaves, or 2 banana leaves

SPECIAL EQUIPMENT

Twine soaked in water (to stop it from burning on the barbecue)

Prepare a medium-high fire in a gas or charcoal grill (or preheat the oven to 350°F/175°C).

To make the masala mixture, heat the coconut oil over medium-high heat in a wide shallow pan, then throw in the curry leaves and mustard seeds. When they start spluttering and popping, add the shallots and ginger.

Stir for a few minutes, until the shallots are softened (but not yet golden), then add the garlic and green chilies. Fry for a couple of minutes, until the raw smell of garlic dissipates.

Add the diced tomatoes to the pan and stir until softened, then add the turmeric, chili powder, coriander powder, and garam masala. Fry for another couple of minutes, until fragrant.

Strain the seeds from the tamarind paste, then add the paste to the pan along with the coconut sugar or jaggery.

Add a few tablespoons of water and cook for around 10 minutes. Add salt to taste. The masala mixture is ready when it's thick, amalgamated, and dark red.

Lay out three overlapping fig leaves and place one fish on top. Season the whole fish lightly with some salt.

Spread a quarter of the masala mixture over the midsection of the fish, then flip the fish over and spread another quarter of the masala on the other side.

Roll the fish up in the leaves (like a burrito!), and tie tightly with the soaked twine.

Repeat with the other fish, using the remaining three fig leaves, some salt, and the remaining masala mixture.

Grill for approximately 10 minutes per side (or roast for 30 minutes in a hot oven). You can tell that the fish is cooked perfectly when it flakes effortlessly from the bone. Gently open up one of the parcels and insert a knife into the flesh to test this.

Embracing Friluftsliv

Scandinavians long ago figured out some very practical habits for well-being that the rest of us are just catching up to—hygge, fika, sauna, for example. Friluftsliv is another one of these concepts. The Norwegian word literally translates to "open-air living"—a way of life practiced year-round by Scandinavians everywhere. This no-fuss, seamless transition between indoor and outdoor life is simply inherent for a large swath of people who could otherwise be quite grumpy about the regularly gray weather. The popular Swedish saying "There is no bad weather, just bad clothes" pretty much sums it up.

What I find especially compelling about friluftsliv is that it fully embraces the knowledge that nature is medicine. Dwelling, playing, communing together in the open air is a healing balm for whatever might ail any of us. Whether we are overworked, sleep-deprived, or simply out of touch with ourselves, nature brings us back to our senses. Spending a lot of time in nature can bring us back to a state of wonder, a childlike frame of mind that delights in the shifting clouds in the sky, a bird alighting on a branch, and, at times, even the feel of pelting rain.

Spending at least five minutes a day in the open air is essential to feeling the effects, and allowing nature to really seep in. You will wish for the sun on your skin every day, and want to feel the hum of outdoor life buzzing around you. You'll discover birds, plants, weather patterns, and trees you never even knew existed.

Whether you live in a city or the country or suburbia, you can always find ways to embrace the open air. Walk instead of driving; choose an outdoor table instead of an inside one; take a bike ride or a hike instead of going to the gym. Spend your weekend or day off at an unexplored outdoor place. Teach your children to love the sun, the clouds, the rain, thunder, snow, but to properly respect them, and know how to enjoy and guard themselves from the perfect power of them all. We don't need to be at war with the elements; instead, we can enter into a beautifully spontaneous dance with Mother Nature where we give and take, push and pull, but, mostly, receive the absolute gift of her healing, clarifying, eye-opening wonders.

Hallie Brewer

Hallie, an artist, maker, and graphic designer, lives in Austin, Texas, her hometown, with her husband, Michael—but they are looking forward to the day they can move into the home they're currently building on family property in the country.

—

Where does your love of the outdoors come from?

Some of my fondest memories from my formative years have nature as the backdrop. Growing up in Austin, I had easy access to parks, natural water spots, and endless activities under the sun. The outdoors was the place to kill time, overcome boredom, and just be with your friends. As an adult, I recognize how valuable it was—and is—to have such access to nature. I was an introverted kid, and nature was a place where I could escape to alone, where I was free to allow my imagination to take over. It still has that effect on me.

What's your relationship with the sun?

The sun's presence, or absence, can greatly affect my moods. Sunshine on my skin can result in instant rejuvenation when I'm feeling low. When the sun is hidden away, I tend toward self-examination and dormancy.

The sun can also provide new inspiration for my art practice. How the sun's light hits a color or casts a shadow onto a shape can give me a new idea for a piece or inform the direction of an existing one.

How do you define well-being? What tangible daily acts do you practice to claim it for yourself?

I define well-being as the relationship one has with their whole self—mind, body, spirit. It's an evolving balance of self-nurturing and self-growth. I believe each person must define these areas for themself. For me, it requires checking in with myself and asking what the nonnegotiables are when it comes to maintaining balance. Recently it's been a combination of journaling, yoga, time spent in nature and with others, lots of laughter, watercoloring, and plenty of rest. Not just quality snoozing, but

shutting out all noise and outside stimulation. Making art can be a great antidote to technology overload.

How has your relationship with the outdoors affected and informed the way you live in your home?

My appreciation for nature and its effect on my well-being means I have as many plants indoors as space allows. I love seeing all the green inside. Throughout my home, you'll find objects collected during my many walks in nature, often from faraway travels. I enjoy living surrounded by these artifacts—like an ever-present travel diary. I like natural light throughout the day; I try not to turn on any artificial lights until the evening. There's a window in my studio that looks into my backyard. I take frequent breaks from whatever I'm working on to observe what's going on outside. It's a refreshing reset for my eyes and mind.

What in nature brings you joy?

The moment when I become fully present in nature, engaging all of my senses. I believe I am the purest, most honest version of myself in these moments.

What are your favorite rituals around food and eating with others?

The potluck is a tried-and-true approach to dining with others. No one person has to carry the full meal responsibility, and everyone gets a chance to show off their skills in the kitchen. My friends are great cooks, so I look forward to tasting their creations. It also usually leads to a recipe exchange by the end of the meal.

What kind of food or meal do you most enjoy sitting down to?

Lately it's been leisurely weekend mornings with my husband, enjoying a spread of breakfast foods, something baked, and ample coffee. It's usually the only meal of the week that isn't rushed.

What activity, habit, or ritual practiced outdoors makes you feel most fully alive and fully yourself?

Lying in the grass facing up toward the sky, day or night.

What environment or place in your childhood or adolescence shaped you most significantly?

The natural Texas landscape—vast, wild, and savage—instilled in me a deep curiosity for mythology, storytelling, and the human need to create meaning within the unknown. The spacious, starry night sky; the sprawling, desolate desert; the deep caverns I explored as a kid all fed my appreciation for the cosmic, the mysterious, the unseen. My childhood interest in these things has spurred a lifelong quest to understand my human place within nature.

How has your time spent outdoors changed as you've gotten older?

Making time to be outdoors, to be with nature, has become a priority as I've gotten older. I work at a computer for many hours of the day. Taking my lunch breaks outside or stepping out for a quick walk around the neighborhood is essential for my mental health.

My husband and I are in the process of building a home on a piece of land about forty miles (sixty kilometers) from the city. We're looking forward to this transition to a more grounding landscape and to the slower pace of life it will afford.

Your collage work and textile pieces are resonant with earth tones and landscape and shape. What have you found influences your work most profoundly?

I'm most influenced by nature (the naturally occurring) and architecture (the human-made) and their coexisting dichotomy. I explore these influences through different mediums and techniques, often through investigating color, form, and material. I believe there's a particular space and feeling I'm trying to get to in my art practice that most closely relates to the experiences I have in nature—stillness, confidence, and serenity. I know it will be a lifelong journey, and I look forward to where it takes me.

—

Rice Noodle Salad

This salad can be made in myriad ways depending on what vegetables and garnishes you have on hand. It's perfect for a light lunch or, with an added protein, such as fried chicken, sautéed shrimp, or baked tofu, a filling dinner.

SERVES 4

DRESSING

¼ cup (60 ml) lime juice

2 tablespoons Thai fish sauce or 1 tablespoon soy sauce

1 teaspoon sugar or honey

2 to 3 teaspoons finely minced ginger

½ teaspoon red pepper flakes

2 tablespoons Asian sesame oil

2 tablespoons canola oil

SALAD

3 ounces (85 g) dried rice vermicelli noodles

½ small Napa cabbage or purple cabbage

½ slivered red, yellow, or green bell pepper

1 medium carrot, grated or cut into fine julienne

3 scallions, thinly sliced

1 cup (40 g) coarsely chopped cilantro

½ cup (70 g) chopped peanuts (optional)

4 cups (160 g) mixed greens of your choice

Mint or basil leaves for garnish (optional)

To make the dressing, mix together the lime juice, fish sauce, sugar, ginger to taste, red pepper flakes, sesame oil, and canola oil in a small bowl or a jar.

To make the salad, bring a large pot of water to a boil. Add the noodles and cook for 1 minute, or until tender. Drain well.

Using scissors, cut the noodles into smaller lengths. Toss with all but 2 tablespoons of the dressing in a large bowl and set aside.

Cut out the core of your cabbage and then slice crosswise into thin strips. Add to the noodles, along with the bell pepper, carrot, scallions, cilantro, and peanuts, if using, and toss to combine.

Line a serving platter with mixed greens and pile on the noodle mixture. Spoon on the remaining dressing. Garnish with mint, if using, and serve.

The core of well-being for me is remembering
to be open to the gift of life.

—Amy Merrick

GATHERING ANYWHERE, ANYTIME

The glorious thing about gathering outdoors is that it can happen almost anywhere, at any time, no reservations or wait times involved. These meetings can be spontaneous or planned, the result of an open invitation or a regular standing date. I like the thought of going to one place as often as you can and arriving with the intention of seeing someone you know each time you go. You may not know who will be there, but you can count on a moment of communion with someone, anyone. Maybe it's a picnic table where you camp out during the weekly farmers' market, or a particular spot in a park with a permanent invitation for fellow dog walkers, other parents with small children, or simply people who like to visit there. Maybe it's the beach you go to on your days off, or the hills not far from your house where you hike. Whatever the spot, whatever the occasion, isn't it lovely to have carefree, agenda-less meetups? The more regularly you see other people, the easier it becomes to cut through the small talk and get to the real stuff.

Best of all, the more often you return to the same place, with the mostly same rotating cast of people, the deeper the sense of belonging you feel there. We all want to *belong*. Belonging to a particular place in nature could be life-changing.

Aliya Wanek

Aliya is a speech therapist for young adults with developmental disabilities. She is the owner/designer of an eponymous earth-aware clothing brand.
—

Where does your love of the outdoors come from?
I think that started when I was a child. I grew up in Florida, where I used to climb up a very big magnolia tree in our front yard and stay there for hours. I had a big imagination, so it just felt like this safe space to be outside and daydream. Also, my family is from Trinidad, so we spent time going to different beaches and fishing—those were part of our family routine.

What's your relationship with the sun?
The sun is energizing. It's something that gives me a bit of a glow. Because of the undertone of my skin, when I'm in the sun a lot, I feel that I shine and brighten. Often there's a feeling that as a Black person, you should not be in the sun so much because you will get darker. Although I've known family members and other people who avoid the sun for that reason, I do not have that insecurity, and I know the vitamin D is good for me.

How do you define well-being and what are some tangible daily acts that you practice to claim that for yourself?
I think well-being is finding equilibrium between your heart, your senses, your instincts, your thoughts. It's also being in touch with your boundaries and how to have those boundaries with people in a loving way where you're not abandoning yourself. Well-being is also being kinder to myself and giving myself the grace to be okay with being me.

Daily things that I do: When I walk my dogs, I walk them in a regular spot, and I really focus on the energy I'm giving to people when I smile and say hi or make small talk. I try to approach people from a sense of warmth, and it's important for me—again stemming from being a Black woman—to be able to have short interactions with people where I can say without actually saying it, I see you in a way that I want you to see me too.

How has your relationship with the outdoors affected and informed the way you live in your home?

I'm drawn to places with lots of windows because I crave a lot of natural light. There's an automatically calming effect from having an abundance of sun.

I've also been trying to bring more plants indoors. My journey with plant life has been going from neglectful to being more intentional about creating a routine and following a schedule to care for them, as I do with my dogs.

What in nature brings you joy?

Lately, I've been noticing a lot of shadow play; the way the sun hits the leaves on the trees. It feels rhythmic, almost like a dance, and that's something I connect with.

I've also been doing a type of somatic-experiencing therapy where it's about taking in the natural world to help reset your system and seeing it as an extension of yourself. I close my eyes and breathe it all in, having a feeling of exchange.

What kind of food or meal do you most enjoy sitting down to?

Curried chicken and roti. My mom will make it, and it's like heaven—roti, oh my gosh. That's my favorite thing.

What's one significant memory or feeling from your childhood surrounding eating with others?

I think it goes back to being seen. Growing up as a Black woman of Caribbean descent, I always felt in between cultures in a sense. With my family, there's such an emphasis on big gatherings; Trinidadians call it *lime*, where you have a lime and that's where you hang out, you eat, you joke, you laugh, and in those moments with my family and with family members visiting from Trinidad, I feel very seen; it helps me feel grounded.

How has your heritage played a part in your experience of community?

Trinidadians, and especially my family, are very good-timey, all about having fun, joking with each other. In my own circle of friends, the more I like you, the more I want to tease you. Any true vision of a gathering has that playful, lively element to it.

What was your relationship to nature as a child, and how has that changed, if at all?

When I was a child sitting in my magnolia tree, it didn't really occur to me how much nature was comforting me. I just did it. But now I'm more aware of the mental health benefits of being in nature, and I'm becoming more appreciative of it.

Especially now that I have my dogs, I've been spending more time outdoors, and growing more acquainted with different places to hike. Having so much access to nature is one of the gems of being in California.

—

Granola with Dried Mango and Chili-Roasted Pistachios

An ideal on-the-go snack for a walk or meetup with a friend any time of day.

MAKES 9 CUPS (JUST OVER 2 L)

⅓ cup (80 ml) maple syrup

⅓ cup (75 g) packed light brown sugar

4 teaspoons vanilla extract

½ teaspoon salt

½ cup (120 ml) vegetable oil

5 cups (450 g) old-fashioned rolled oats

1 cup (130 g) chili-roasted pistachios, coarsely chopped

½ cup (60 g) cashews, coarsely chopped

¾ cup (100 g) pumpkin seeds

½ cup (75 g) sesame seeds

½ cup (70 g) sunflower seeds

2 cups (320 g) bite-sized pieces dried mango

Preheat the oven to 325°F (165°C). Whisk the maple syrup, brown sugar, vanilla, and salt together in a large bowl. Whisk in the oil. Fold in the oats, nuts, and seeds until thoroughly coated.

Transfer the oat mixture to a parchment paper–lined rimmed baking sheet and spread it into a thin, even layer (about ⅜ inch/10 mm thick). Using a wide spatula, press on the mixture to compact it.

Bake, rotating the pan halfway through baking, until the granola is lightly browned, 40 to 45 minutes. Remove the granola from the oven and let cool to room temperature on the baking sheet (about 1 hour).

Break the cooled granola into pieces of the desired size and transfer to a bowl. Stir in the pieces of dried mango. (*The granola can be stored in an airtight container at room temperature for up to 2 weeks.*)

There's no better feeling than diving into the water and swimming as far as you want.

Hannah Ferrara

Being Well Under the Sun

Dr. Lena Dicken is a clinical psychologist and a nature lover. Her past research, as well as her current ongoing work, is centered on the inextricable links between personal well-being and the time we spend outdoors, soaking up the natural world.

—

You've done a lot of research on the connection between time spent in nature and its effects on mental/physical/spiritual well-being. What has been the most significant or, perhaps, personal finding of your research?

I spent about six years during my twenties living, working, and traveling around the world in search of some of the most beautiful and awe-inspiring places in nature. At the conclusion of my travels, I reflected on my experience with both immense gratitude and the realization that something profound had shifted within me. I felt, at my core, a happier person.

I knew that although that chapter of my life was ending and a new, more structured academic one was beginning, I was eager to deepen my understanding of what I had experienced. When I first began graduate school and set out to research the connections between nature and well-being, I was struck by the many studies that confirmed my hunch about my experiences. It turned out that experiencing awe, as when we're watching the sun set, riding a wave, or standing in the presence of a waterfall, has been proven to increase prosocial behaviors, reduce cortisol in the body, and increase subjective well-being. In other words, spending more time in nature means you're more likely to empathize with and give more to others, as well as to feel calmer, more peaceful, and happier.

Given the high rate of anxiety and depression in our hyperconnected world, these findings have profound implications for humanity at large, especially when you take into account the concept of neuroplasticity, which is the brain's ability to adapt and grow by creating new neural networks. That process also reshapes existing neural networks and can even eliminate existing networks if they're no longer being used. Essentially, our environment, culture, emotions, and perceptions are reshaping our brains every day. This means that how, where, and whom we spend our time with have significant effects on our well-being.

What have you found in your own life and in your psychology practice to be the most profound source of healing when it comes to activities, rituals, or rhythms around time spent in nature?

The most profound experiences of healing have come when I'm fully present in nature. Too often we're caught up in our own thoughts and the constant chatter in our heads, which means we're taking in only a limited experience of our surroundings. To help myself become more present, I always try to focus on all my senses when I'm in nature. I begin by taking a few deep breaths. First to calm my nervous system and relax, then to smell the air and the scents around me. Living in Santa Barbara, I can almost always smell something amazing, whether it's the ocean or the forest, desert sage or wildflowers. Next I scan my surroundings and really see what's around me. I look at the color of the sky and how the light is hitting the things in my field of vision. I notice any sensations I'm experiencing, such as the wind on my skin or the warmth of the sun on my face. I take note of any sounds nearby, like the breeze rustling the trees or the birds chirping. And I pay attention to the temperature and the way my body feels depending on how warm or cool it is.

Lately I've also been spending time reflecting on the Indigenous peoples who previously inhabited the land where I find myself. That perspective was missing for me for many years, and it's been a grounding process as well as a recurring act of respect that is important to acknowledge.

Your practice incorporates mindfulness as a key tool for cultivating well-being. What's the most helpful or illuminating way you've found to describe mindfulness to clients and how it can help them?

Mindfulness is being present and observing what's happening without judgment. As we go through our lives, to be mindful is to be aware. When we're practicing mindfulness, we're paying attention both to what's happening in life around us and to what's going on internally. To be mindful of the external world can mean tuning in to your senses, or really listening when you're having a conversation with someone, without jumping in to respond. To be mindful internally means to pay attention to your feelings and internal dialogue.

What do you find to be particularly useful advice from the wellness world? What is better left ignored?

There's so much advice from the wellness world that at times it can feel overwhelming. In my opinion, one downside of the wellness world is that it often feels like it's selling me something—a new workout tool, a treatment, an app, a powder, a superfood. I think the things that really nourish our bodies don't cost a lot of money: They are things like moving our bodies every day, getting enough sleep, resting when we're tired, eating fresh foods, and practicing relaxation techniques like meditation or breathing exercises.

What's one simple, practical bit of advice for someone looking to explore or perhaps deepen the mind-body connection?

Any practice that connects the breath and the body would be a good place to start. Some examples include yoga, which is great for strengthening the body while connecting to the breath, and tai chi, which is low-impact exercise that connects the breath to slow, meditative movements. I also often recommend breathing exercises as a way to reduce stress and anxiety. Anxiety is often accompanied by shallow breathing, so by paying attention to your breath and focusing on deep breathing in the diaphragm, you can actually slow your heart rate and lower and stabilize your blood pressure. Diaphragmatic breathing also activates the vagus nerve, which is the nerve that triggers your body's relaxation response (the parasympathetic nervous system) and lowers your body's stress response (the sympathetic nervous system).

What are some meaningful—therapeutic, even—ways that people can spend time in nature that go beyond just a walk or sunbathing?

Besides reaping the benefits of the outdoors while doing activities they enjoy, I often encourage people to give back to nature in some way: for example, by participating in community gardening, picking up trash, volunteering with animals, or planting trees in their neighborhood. Participating in these activities can help build a two-way relationship with nature that can help you feel good on multiple levels.

What's a common piece of advice you give to your clients? Or what's a common question you ask them?

One of the most common things I discuss with my clients is their inner dialogue. Many people have a very harsh inner critic, which ends up getting in the way of their self-confidence and self-esteem. Once I ask them to start paying attention to that, there's often a realization that there's a lot of room to extend more kindness and compassion to themselves. This takes work, but it often results in their achieving more peace and calm in their lives.

Hannah Ferrara and Malcolm Smitley

This North Carolina couple swapped out their Southern home for the rivers and forests of the Pacific Northwest, where Hannah continues her long-time craft of metalsmithing through her jewelry line, Another Feather, and Malcolm practices his love of cooking as a professional chef.

—

Where does your love of the outdoors come from?

Hannah: Right after I was born, my parents took me out to the beach in my bassinet, so you could quite literally say I spent the beginning of my life outdoors. To this day, I can fall asleep instantly out by the ocean, or on any boat, to the sound of waves.

Malcolm: When I was growing up in the South, my dad used to take us camping, and he taught us the importance of sitting in nature, to always "take in the sounds, smells, and sights." Learning to become intimate with those details of the woods was really foundational for me, and sitting in stillness is something I continue to practice now when I'm outdoors.

What's your relationship with the sun?

H: I am a total sun-worshipper—which has been the hardest part of living in the Pacific Northwest, where a chunk of the year is damp and dark. I've learned a lot from Scandinavians about how to "hygge," but honestly, I need to find the sun somewhere to get through the winter, even if that just means taking a day trip to the desert now and then. Then it's pure late-summer bliss here with long, warm days and sun every day, and we spend every moment we can outside in it to build up a reserve for the winter months.

How do you define well-being? What tangible daily acts do you practice to claim it for yourself?

H: The definition has changed as I've grown and come into my own. Lately my daily practices include quieting my mind and reading in the morning to center my perspective for the day, getting outside, drinking tons of water, putting away my phone, investing in others, and moving my body.

What in nature brings you joy?

M: The overwhelming sense of peace found there.

H: Release. Being able to put aside obligations and responsibilities and just be there. Then there's the pure beauty of it. To me, nothing human-made can compare.

How has your relationship with the outdoors affected and informed the way you live in your home?

H: Our home tends to reflect our love of the natural world in our general ethos around living and bringing aspects of the outdoors inside. First and foremost, allowing as much natural light in as possible; then, using natural materials and palettes, plants, and fireplaces, both indoors and out, where we spend much of our time. We are very lucky to have multiple outdoor areas at our house, including a large front porch and a back patio, and when the weather is nice, the doors are always open and we spend the majority of our mornings and evenings out there. There are also random collections of items gathered over the years from nature that serve as curios in our home: stones and pebbles, driftwood, shells, and dried flowers, to name a few.

What do you find to be the true value of gathering around food with friends?

M: Food can bring people from completely different backgrounds and cultures together and, literally, give everyone a seat at the table. I was a shy kid, but joining in a meal with others felt like a comfortable and approachable way to have a conversation, meet someone, and open up without pressure. As an adult who has worked with food most of my life, that is still my favorite aspect of a meal—bringing people together and watching conversations unfold naturally.

What are your favorite rituals around food and eating with others?

H: I love to snap a photograph of the tablescape afterward; the beautiful mess after a long dinner—dirty plates, half-empty wineglasses, crumpled cloth napkins. There is so much memory in that.

What kind of food or meal do you most enjoy sitting down to?

M: A simple but comforting meal prepared outdoors, such as seasonal vegetables cooked over the fire and a spit-roasted chicken.

H: I love a long picnic. No chairs, just lounging on blankets, but pulling out all the stops. A full smorgasbord of everything: platters and boards, cloth napkins, Duralex glassware. My essentials—oysters, olives, dates, various spreads, tinned sardines, bread, an assortment of goat and sheep cheeses, fresh figs from our tree, grain salads, whatever fruit is in season, and almond cake for dessert, with multiple bottles of natural wine. An ideal scenario is a picnic that takes place by the ocean and ends with a crab feast for dinner. My favorite meal in the world is a whole steamed crab drenched in lemon juice.

What's one significant memory or feeling from your childhood surrounding eating with others?

H: I have a big mixed Italian American New York family on my dad's side, and I have fond memories of us all sitting together at the longest of tables eating Sunday pasta with homemade red sauce that had simmered all day.

My mother's side is on the Southern coast, and my grandmother would always make a huge shrimp boil. The whole family sits around peeling and eating shrimp until everyone is stuffed and someone volunteers to throw all the shells in the canal. I still have that meal every time I go home.

M: Camping with my dad, when he would cook in a Dutch oven over the fire. I think that shaped my own love for cooking outdoors over a fire, and for eating outside in general.

You have a free day to do absolutely whatever you want, as long as it's spent outdoors. How do you fill your time?

H: We would start by going to the farmers' market in the morning and gathering fresh produce and picnic provisions. If it's summer, we always head to the water

(either the coast or the river) and spend the day swimming and reading, then go home to make dinner on our back patio, take an evening stroll, and linger on the patio. If it's winter or spring, sub a long afternoon hike in the forest for swimming.

How did growing up in lush North Carolina shape your relationship to nature? What has carried over to your life in Oregon?

H: Both of us spent the majority of our childhoods outdoors, whether in the woods or at the beach, and that instilled an appreciation of nature early on, as well as a need for continuing a lifelong relationship with it. Living in North Carolina gave us access to so many diverse terrains all in one place, and Oregon felt like the West Coast version of this. In both places, you can live in the city and day-trip to the ocean, mountains, river, forest, or farmlands. It's one of the aspects we love most about both places, and it's why Oregon easily felt like home.

Hannah, I know that things found in nature routinely inspire your jewelry collections. What are some recurring themes for you?

Shells, ocean forms, mountains, orchid petals, and water are all recurring natural themes that reappear throughout my collections. Textures and patterns found in nature more subtly inspire me; that can be seen in something as simple as a hammered pattern that references birchbark.

Malcolm, given that your career and vocation center around food and cooking for others, how do you approach cooking differently when it's just for fun at home on your own and/or with friends—if, in fact, there is a shift for you?

For me, cooking is always first about the people and then about the food. Most of the time I approach cooking for work no differently than I do cooking for friends or family, though the latter is a bit more laid-back, of course. When making a meal at home, I like to get everyone involved in the process. The cooking can be more spontaneous, and I delegate tasks like chopping, peeling, and plating so that everyone has a hand in the meal.

What out-of-doors activity or activities make you feel like a kid again, in the best way possible?

H: Swimming. I spent much of my childhood swimming, so it will always have that connection for me, and, hopefully, will continue to keep me young.

M: Rock climbing and scrambling over boulders.

What type of nature setting gives you the most at-ease sensation?

H: Water, always. Ocean first, then rivers. To me, there's no better feeling than diving into the water and swimming as far as you want, or just floating freely.

M: The forest and the desert. The desert always makes it clear how vast the world is and how small we are in comparison, and those wide-open spaces can help put our human problems in perspective. The forest makes me feel hugged by nature. The soft forest floor and a canopy of trees above cradle you in growth.

—

Ember-Kissed Grilled Whole Fish

Perfectly prepared fish is only partly about the cooking; the key is to start by finding the freshest local fish possible. In the Pacific Northwest, we have an abundance of options depending on the season, but I can always count on getting wild salmon, trout, or sablefish. For this out-of-town occasion, we stopped at the fish docks in Santa Barbara to pick up branzino on our way out to camp.

Almost any small to medium-sized whole fish will work here. The number of servings will depend on the size of the fish, but a 1- to 2-pound fish (455 to 900 g) will serve 2 or 3. This is less of a recipe and more of a technique for cooking whole fish in the simplest, most delicious way with fire. You can also garnish the grilled fish with more herbs. Serve with a large salad, grilled bread, and grilled vegetables.

Whole branzino, cleaned and scaled

Salt and pepper

Lemon slices

1 bunch parsley

Thyme sprigs

Rosemary sprigs

Olive oil, for brushing and drizzling (the best you can find, for optimal flavor)

Lemon wedges for garnish (optional)

The first thing to do is build a fire. I prefer cooking with a wood fire (local wood is best), but charcoal works too. Once the fire is going, you are looking for red-hot coals and little to no smoke for cooking. While the fire is warming up, gather your ingredients and prepare the fish.

Season the inside of the fish with salt and pepper and stuff it with lemon slices and herbs (and anything else you've found for flavor). If your fish is on the larger side, you may need to carefully tie it closed with butcher's twine, making sure not to tear the skin.

When the fire is nice and hot, brush the outside of the fish with olive oil and lay it on the grill. Let the fish cook for 5 to 8 minutes on each side depending on the size of your fish and the heat of the fire. The skin should get crispy and slightly charred. When the fish is cooked on the first side, flip and repeat. Using tongs, pull the fish off the fire when it looks perfectly ember kissed, transfer to a platter, and drizzle with olive oil. Serve with lemon wedges, if desired.

THINGS TO DO OUTSIDE WITH A FRIEND

Getting tired of looking at your phones together? Try one or two or three of these activities—you'll feel so much better.

~ Take a walk.

~ Bask in the sun.

~ Find a body of water and play in it like your eight-year-old self.

~ Seed a pile of pomegranates (into a bowl of water is best).

~ Listen to the birds.

~ Take a nap.

~ Drink lemonade.

~ Eat a sandwich.

~ Read a book out loud.

~ Look at some magazines.

~ Tell stories from childhood.

~ Draw or watercolor.

~ Kick, throw, or lob a ball back and forth.

~ Dance.

~ Ask the questions you're waiting to be asked.

~ Daydream.

~ Play cards.

~ Cook something over a fire.

~ Pick a wildflower bouquet.

~ Take a bike ride.

~ Write postcards.

~ Collect something.

~ Watch the sunset.

~ Take a rambling drive.

~ Fly a kite.

~ Plant something.

~ Rake leaves, shovel snow, or tackle a cleaning project.

~ Sit somewhere to people-watch and tell stories (kind ones) about the people you see.

~ Stargaze.

~ Do a stoop-sit (or porch, fire escape, backyard . . . whatever your equivalent).

~ Stretch.

~ Talk about your hopes and dreams.

~ Do a puzzle.

Trilby Nelson

Trilby is a designer who conceptualizes and creates exhibits for a number of museums in the Santa Fe area, and also designs blankets—and other textiles—ideal for an instantly cheery picnic anywhere you land.

—

What in nature brings you joy?
Beauty and quiet.

What tangible daily acts do you practice to claim well-being for yourself?
Meditating, taking long walks with my dog, and connecting with family and friends keep me balanced and happy.

How has your relationship with the outdoors affected and informed the way you live in your home?
I like to bring the outdoors inside with lots of natural light and open windows and doors.

What are your favorite rituals around food and eating with others?
A picnic with friends or a home-cooked meal with family.

What's one significant memory or feeling from your childhood surrounding eating with others?
Camping in the Sierras with cousins: my dad barbecuing ribs all day long, eating corn on the cob, and enjoying watermelon that had been chilled in the ice-cold river.

How has living in the desert changed the way you experience nature or, perhaps, the way you interact with the landscape?
I've found that I'm in nature more here than anywhere else I've lived because the high-desert climate makes it easy and enjoyable to be outside during every season. Living here has also made me realize how fragile and susceptible to drought, wildfires, and other effects of climate change the desert is.

Is there a specific place (or places) in nature you like to retreat to that makes you feel most grounded and down-to-earth?
Hiking among the ponderosa pines in the Sangre de Cristo Mountains that surround Santa Fe.

What does a summer morning feel, smell, sound, and look like in Santa Fe?
Cool, crisp air; bright sunshine; and the warm smell of ponderosa, piñon, and willow trees.

How do you most often choose to play outdoors at this stage of your life?
Neighborhood walks or mountain hikes with my dog.

Where do you look to when you need a bit more clear-headedness and perspective on life?
A walk or swim usually does the trick.

What's your favorite scent in nature that immediately transports you to a different time and place?
Two scents in particular send me straight back to my childhood in Los Angeles. A whiff of eucalyptus or rose instantly evokes memories of playing in my grand-mothers' abundant and lush gardens.

—

Summer Lemon Cream Tart

Perfect for a summer picnic or almost any occasion, special or ordinary.

SERVES 4 TO 8

CRUST

1¼ cups (155 g) flour

3 tablespoons (38 g) sugar

½ teaspoon (3 g) salt

8 tablespoons (1 stick/113 g) butter

3 to 4 tablespoons (45 to 60 ml) ice water

FILLING

8 ounces (225 g) cream cheese, softened

¼ cup (50 g) sugar

Grated zest and juice of 1 lemon
(approximately 2 tablespoons juice)

TOPPING

2 to 3 cups (280 to 420 g) whole berries or sliced stone fruit

GLAZE

2 tablespoons lemon juice

2 tablespoons sugar

To make the crust, combine the flour, sugar, and salt in a medium bowl. Cut the butter into the flour mixture until the butter is the size of peas. Add just enough ice water so the dough comes together.

Turn the dough out and shape it into a disk. Wrap in parchment paper and chill for 30 to 45 minutes.

Preheat the oven to 375°F (190°C). Remove the dough from the refrigerator and let sit at room temperature for 5 minutes.

On a floured surface, roll the dough out into a 12-inch (30 cm) round and fit it in a 9-inch (23 cm) tart pan, pressing it over the bottom and up the sides. Trim off any excess dough with a sharp knife. Line the tart shell with foil and fill it with dried beans or rice.

Bake the crust for 10 minutes, then remove the foil and beans or rice. Prick the crust all over with a fork and bake for another 20 minutes, or until lightly brown. Remove from the oven and let the crust cool completely.

To make the filling, combine the cream cheese, sugar, and lemon zest and juice in a bowl and beat until smooth. Spread evenly over the cooled crust.

Top the filling with the berries or fruit.

To make the glaze, combine the lemon juice and sugar in a small saucepan and heat over low heat, stirring, until the sugar has dissolved and the glaze has thickened. Remove from the heat and let cool.

To serve, gently brush the glaze over the fruit. Enjoy!

The Peace of Pause

Being outdoors is the invitation to slowness we all crave. Nature is our ultimate teacher in showing us that things take the time they need. Nothing is hurried; nothing is delayed. For instance, observe the birds. Sit in a chair or lie on the grass and let them come. Hang a feeder and watch them eat; how carefully they find just what they need. To watch a bird—to slow down and observe a wren or a heron or a hawk in all its glory—is to practice perhaps the easiest, most accessible kind of meditation. It is getting outside of one's own thoughts to see how another being lives. What is simpler or more satisfying than seeing other creatures be completely their creaturely selves? There is deep comfort in being reminded that wildlife live in the moment—unselfconsciously, presumably without worry.

Repose can be found not only in sitting, watching, and waiting, but also by engaging in activities during which we tend not to judge ourselves. These are rituals that give our minds a rest—slow, methodical acts involving attention to a seemingly mindless task: raking leaves, pulling weeds, hanging laundry in the sun. If we give our full awareness to the project at hand, we find the gift of pause from our need for productivity. Yes, the plants need to be watered, but this variety of to-do ranks quite differently in our minds than, say, emptying the in-box. This simple engagement with nature gives us the raw sense of being fully ourselves again, without feeling like nothing more than a tiny cog in the wheels of society, endlessly turning round and round without reprieve.

The peace we find in wild things—in beings and practices out in nature—is perhaps the same sensation we have when floating in water. We become like children again, with childlike fervor and bodily freedom.

Submerging ourselves in water—whether a river, a pond, the ocean, or an outdoor tub—can bring us back to our elemental selves. Doesn't dipping under the surface feel a little like waking up anew? Coming up for air, we are cleansed and revived. Every. Single. Time.

If you don't know what I mean, get yourself to a body of water and let yourself go. Let yourself lie there, heavy in the water, arms outspread. Sink down for a moment if you need to. Water, whether hot or cold, shocks us back into our deepest senses and sensations, letting everything else peel away for a time. It's this peeling away that gives us the pause we need from the cult of busyness, the endless thrum of civilization vying for our attention, our earnings, our loyalty. What a relief it would be if we were accountable only to nature and to our complete enjoyment of it, to our total tranquility within it.

The outdoors waits patiently for you. Whenever you need a long interlude from the song and dance of life, nature offers herself to you, freely, to rest in and recharge. To remind you of how small, how capable, how human each one of us is. The gift of calm is lingering just beyond your walls. Be kind to yourself and go find it.

Amy Merrick and Philip Shelley

Amy is a writer and florist who currently lives in London with her architect husband, Philip. Amy unveils her rich symbiosis with every little bit of the outdoors.
—

Where does your love of the outdoors come from?
My family has a very unified and worshipful relationship to nature. Surely all those childhood days spent rambling around in the woods and meadows are to blame for my continual longing to be outside.

What's your relationship with the sun?
I probably photosynthesize just like a leaf, getting lots of energy from the sun. Although if I were a plant, I'd definitely be in the part-shade category—I'm quick to wilt in the heat. A place in dappled shade is far and away my preferred picnic spot.

How do you define well-being? What tangible daily acts do you practice to claim it for yourself?
The core of well-being for me is remembering to be open to the gift of life. It comes in waves, but taking long baths helps, and so does talking with my sister often, even if she is thousands of miles away.

How has your relationship with the outdoors affected and informed the way you live in your home?
Flowers everywhere, very simply arranged and entirely unfussy, plucked from the grocery store or my garden or an obliging roadside. We light a fire in the fireplace far more often than is strictly necessary, making the whole house smell earthy and woodsy, and I shuffle pots of herbs and flowers back and forth between the garden and table. There is a fine line between outdoors and in; just open up the windows, and everything is one.

What do you find to be the true value of gathering around food with friends?
I think eating with friends, and especially cooking for friends, is nourishing emotionally and physically. Feeding someone with care is an easy way to show them you love them.

What in nature brings you joy?

New buds on my geraniums, pruning roses, dandelions' puffs, sunset walks, morning coffee in my garden, sidewalks shiny with rain, spiderwebs strung with dew, fruit ripening on the trees.

What are your favorite rituals around food and eating with others?

Setting the table and lighting candles are a must; we do it no matter the meal. My idea of heaven would be drawers full of fancy beeswax taper candles that I could burn low every night.

Where is the most pleasure for you in food? Growing it? Preparing it? Sharing it with others?

The creativity and improvisation of using ingredients I already have on hand to make something beautiful is so satisfying and one of my greatest joys in the kitchen. And I can never help myself with the little flourishes that make things feel gently luxurious: fresh herbs scattered, curls of zest, clouds of Parm or flower petals. That food looks appetizing and inviting is so important to enjoying it.

What kind of food or meal do you most enjoy sitting down to?

An early dinner, around five or six, is such a pleasure. There's lots of time to savor the meal, and lots of time afterward to unwind from the day. A walk after dinner is a wonderful thing.

What's one significant memory or feeling from your childhood surrounding eating with others?

When the lettuce came into my dad's garden, I remember we ate so much salad that we would go through a bottle of dressing in a day. There was no struggle over vegetables at home; we didn't have a choice. On Thanksgiving, my mom would play a game called "count the vegetables." We'd often have eight or nine different varieties on the table.

Your work with both flowers and words has a beautiful sensitivity and lightness—where do you think that sensibility comes from?

With flowers, I gravitate more and more to ones that feel entirely unstudied; belaboring an arrangement zaps it of spirit. In writing, the most frank and natural words similarly feel the best.

What's your favorite form of play at this stage of your life?

After many itinerant years, I am loving setting up a home, sewing and knitting, painting, creating, cooking, collecting things, and generally bathing in domesticity at every turn.

Where do you find the most profound sense of rest?

My family's summerhouse in New Hampshire puts me at ease like nowhere else. It's my cocoon, where I feel close to the generations who were there before me.

As we get older, forming new friendships seems to get infinitely harder. Where have you found your greatest sense of connection and community in recent years?

It is both a blessing and a curse to have best friends scattered to the wind. I feel like I've left bits of my heart all over the world and that I have to go back to visit to feel whole again. Making a home of our own in London, though, feels so right. It is a place where flowers and gardens hold a deep, cultural value unlike any I've found elsewhere.

Do you have any habits or routines around spending time in nature that make you feel especially grounded and at peace?

It may sound absurdly simple, but it's an amazing thing to spend time outside alone; no books or phones or other distractions, just sitting in one spot and looking, even if only for a few minutes: clouds passing overhead, branches swaying, ants crawling. It completely resets my mood and mind, and my sense of time.

—

Undone Cheesecake

With swaths of cream and fruit and buttery cookie crumbles, this effortless deconstructed cheesecake was inspired by the chefs at my favorite London restaurant, Ducksoup. My version was adapted from Clare Lattin and Tom Hill's brilliant Ducksoup Cookbook: The Wisdom of Simple Cooking. *Their recipe calls for Brillat-Savarin, that gorgeous French triple-cream cheese, in place of humble Philadelphia brand, but at our summerhouse in New Hampshire, we work with what we can get from the local grocery store and then up the ante with handpicked berries.*

SERVES 2

½ cup (65 g) crushed almond cookies or digestive biscuits

1½ tablespoons (20 g) butter

3½ ounces (100 g) cream cheese, softened

3 tablespoons (40 g) crème fraîche, at room temperature

⅓ cup (70 g) Greek yogurt, at room temperature

½ cup (100 g) mascarpone, at room temperature

A few drops of lemon juice

Seasonal fruit for garnish

Toasted nuts for garnish

Put the crushed cookies in a small saucepan, add the butter, and gently heat the mixture, stirring, until the butter melts and the crumbs are evenly moistened. Remove from the heat and refrigerate until chilled.

Put the cream cheese, crème fraîche, yogurt, mascarpone, and lemon juice in a medium bowl and stir until just combined; do not overmix.

To assemble, spread the cheese mixture on a serving plate and top with fruit, the cookie crumbles, and toasted nuts. Serve immediately.

Hana Taninaka-Lee

Hana, her husband, Jeremy Lee, and their four kids live on the Far North Coast of New South Wales, Australia, where Hana runs a company called Taninaka that makes organic bed linens for children and Jeremy builds fine handcrafted furniture.

—

Where does your love of the outdoors come from?
It's always been there, but as I have gotten older, it's something I have dived deeper into, almost like shedding a skin to tap back into the connection to nature that we all are born with. I find sharing this joy of nature with my children magical—watching them pick fruit, or seeing their excitement about a seedling popping up, or their absolute gusto when walking through thick, dense bush as I carefully follow them. It's all joy.

What's your relationship with the sun?
The sun is my life force. It directs all my actions. Finding the sunny spot where I can sit and eat my breakfast, crossing the road to walk on the bright side of the street, watching what the sunlight does to the trees when I'm driving. Watching what the sunlight does to everything, really. The feeling of sitting in the winter sun and peeling off all your layers, stretching out, and letting your skin drink it all in. The summer sun brings out a youthfulness, a freeness. A memory of road trips and long days doing nothing, or of balmy evenings with people you love. Thinking of the sun, you can't help but smile. Sun, sun, I love you!

How has your relationship with the outdoors affected and informed the way you live in your home?
We get "the northerlies" in summer; when we came and looked at the house before buying it, I felt the wind and had a feeling of coming home on a summer evening after a day at the beach. It was like a memory from our future, and I knew then that this place was our home.

We let the light in anywhere we can—no curtains—so it pours in all day long. Where the light hits the house is where we will find ourselves. We have passion fruit vines growing wild around the deck. The kids run out and pick the fruit as soon as it's turned the slightest shade of purple; they can't wait until it's really ready and

ripe. We have a giant daybed on the deck positioned so we can laze in the sunshine all day while the kids run wild in the garden. We have shovels and spades and ladders and ropes and saws—ready for the kids to dig, pick, climb, cut. The garden is their own adventureland.

What do you find to be the true value of gathering around food with friends?

I think there is so much love in eating with friends; food is such an expression of love, and for me, food is life. The table is where we sit down and share about our day; it's where we show care through baking a birthday cake, or making someone their favorite breakfast; it's sitting with friends and laughing—or crying. Bringing food to a new mama or a sick friend. Having my sister and her kids over for dinner because it's easier to handle the chaos when we're together. For me, sharing food is about living life together.

What in nature brings you joy?

The other day I was in the water and a single droplet was hanging from my eyelash. It was mesmerizing. It's those magic moments that blow my mind—these little windows into this crazy universe we live in, tapping into the magic that surrounds us.

What kind of food or meal do you most enjoy sitting down to?

It would either be a delicious teishoku—crispy salmon, rice, miso soup, and pickles—or a giant bowl of saucy pasta with heaps of Parmesan and chili flakes. Any Japanese meal really is so comforting to me. Each pregnancy, all I wanted to do was eat Japanese food, and any time I'm sick, all I want is an okaiyu (Japanese rice porridge). It's home food for me. And pasta is a forever love. Plus cake—I always, always love cake.

How has having children changed or deepened your experience of nature? What things are your kids teaching you or teaching you again about how to be fully present in your environment?

I think of that saying, "We are not on the earth, we are of the earth." Having kids awakens us to the notion that we are not separate from nature, that we are a part of it. When I look at my children in nature, there is so much connection; they are completely in it. Whenever our twin girls are upset in the middle of the night, we come to them and look at the moon and the stars. With all our babies, it has been like this. Being under the moon, feeling the night air, and looking at all the stars—it really drops you in. An immediate calm.

What's your favorite scent found in nature that immediately transports you to a different time and place?

Jasmine in the springtime. The house I grew up in had jasmine growing all along the front fence.

What kind of landscape or environment makes you feel most wild and free?

Out in the surf, when it's windy and a bit rough, a bit cloudy—it feels raw and wild and I absolutely love it. It takes me out of mind completely and washes me about. Or anytime surfing, really, when I am immersed in the water, I feel free. It is transporting and invigorating and revitalizing all at once. It's a place just for me, and a place for everyone else too. Surfing—it's pure fun, pure freedom.

What gives you hope lately?

Community. I think there has been a great reconnection to community for a lot of people. It is such a beautiful thing—a better understanding of your own environment, your impact on it, and of the others living within it, and how everyone can work together toward its well-being as a whole. It's a beautiful symbiosis.

—

Damper on a Stick

This recipe is one we would make when we were camping growing up. However, bush damper has been made by Aboriginals for tens of thousands of years. I would like to acknowledge here the Traditional Custodians of the land I live and raise my children on, the Arakwal people of Bundjalung Nation, and pay my respects to Elders past and present. I recognize their continued connection to the land and waters of this incredible place and thank them for their ongoing protection of this beautiful coastline and all the ecosystems within it. I recognize that First Nations sovereignty was never ceded. This continent always was and always will be Aboriginal land.

MAKES 4 TO 6 DAMPERS

2 cups (250 g) self-rising flour

2 tablespoons (28 g) butter, plus more for serving

2 teaspoons (8 g) sugar

Pinch of salt

¾ cup (180 ml) water

Honey for serving

Begin by building a fire and collecting long, narrow but sturdy sticks for toasting your dampers. Make sure you use sticks from nontoxic trees or bushes.

Put the flour in a medium bowl and rub the butter into it until you have a crumbly mixture.

Mix in the sugar and salt. Slowly add the water, mixing until a dough forms. Knead the dough for a minute or two until it holds together and is smooth.

Divide the dough into 4 to 6 balls, depending on how big you want your dampers. Roll each ball into a snake.

Coil the dough around your sticks: Start at the point of each stick and fold the dough over it, then coil it around the stick one layer at a time until you reach a length of 5 to 7 inches (13 to 18 cm), or until your dough runs out.

Toast the dampers over the fire (toasting over the hot embers is better than using the flame) until they are nice and crunchy on the outside and sound kind of hollow when you tap them.

Pull the dampers off the sticks and fill them with butter and honey to serve.